Mrs. Allen

ON All FOURS

Develop the Perfect Relationship with Your Pet

Barbara A. Allen

The advice contained in this book is based on my own experience with animals and that of professionals with whom I've been privileged to consult, and is not intended to substitute for the advice of a qualified veterinarian. Only your veterinarian can recommend what's best for your dog or cat where diet or health are concerned. Regular veterinary visits are an important part of caring for your pet.

Produced and published by
Regency Press, Farmington Connecticut

Design by Carolyn Bligh, Bligh Graphics
Simsbury, Connecticut

Library of Congress Catalog Card Number: 99-066921

ISBN: 0-9673264-0-0

First Printing: October 1999

Photography credits:
Provost Photography, Christopher Provost
Richard Crane

This book is dedicated to my passionate and supportive husband and my incredibly loving daughters.

This book is also in memory of Jano, my German Shepherd, who at the time of this writing is dying. If more humans had his values, honor and unconditional love, the world would be a lovely and harmonious place to live.

— Barbara Allen

With thanks to Elizabeth Michalski for all of her
hard work on this project.

CONTENTS

FOREWORD   7

INTRODUCTION   11

1. Developing the Perfect Relationship   15

2. Communication Is Key   29

3. Genetics = Purpose and Potential   43

4. The Power of Positive Training   57

5. Working With Your Veterinarian   75

6. Nutrition, Nutrition, Nutrition   87

7. Stepping Out   101

8. De-Stressing Your Pet   115

9. Travel Time   133

10. Holiday Hangovers   145

FOREWORD

Michael Good, DVM

As a veterinarian who runs four clinics in Atlanta, I've seen more than my fair share of skin and shedding problems in pets. I've had owners come to me in tears because their allergies to a dog's coat are so bad they have to get rid of him. I've had others tell me how much they'd love to have a cat, but that they just can't deal with the shedding. And I've never had anything to offer my clients that would help.

Two years ago I was paging through a national magazine when I saw a piece about Mrs. Allen's SHED-STOP. I'd seen products like these before, and they never delivered on their promises. I was immediately skeptical, so I gave Barbara a call, intending to disprove her claims. She graciously offered to send me a case of SHED-STOP, and I shared it with my clients.

Within a month, I had owners coming into my clinics raving about the stuff — how their dog had virtually stopped shedding, how their cat's skin had improved, how happy their children were now that they could finally have a pet of their own. I've been a firm believer in SHED-STOP — and in Barbara — ever since.

Eventually, I got to know Barbara personally, and I've been nothing but impressed. She is a wonderful woman who truly

cares about animals, and manages to still see the human side of
the pet/owner equation as well. She recognizes the important
role that dogs and cats play in today's families. She wants them
to be as healthy and happy as possible so they — and their
owners — can spend more time enjoying each other.

This book is an expression of Barbara's desire to help pets
and people get along better. It contains lots of practical advice
and wisdom on how to make the most out of your relationship
with your dog or cat. Whether you are a long-time pet owner,
or someone who has recently bonded for the first time with a
puppy or kitten, use this "owner's manual" to make the path to
a perfect relationship smoother and easier for both of you.

— Michael Good, DVM

INTRODUCTION

Barbara Allen

Whenever a new animal comes to live with me, the first thing I do is kneel down on the floor and try to see my house from his perspective. What objects seem dangerous or scary? What type of trouble can he get into, and how can I prevent it? What areas look safe and inviting? What is the dog or cat likely to think of his new environment?

For me, taking the time to see life from a pet's perspective is natural. I've been around animals all my life — my family raised dogs, I've shown my pets in all different disciplines, and I've ridden horses competitively for years. I never could have succeeded in these different areas if I hadn't developed a partnership with my pets.

Not everyone has been lucky enough to spend days at a time just observing how their pet acts and thinks, and not everyone is confident about the best way to raise a pet. Some people are just starting out with a new puppy or kitten and want to make sure they start the relationship right; others may have an older dog or cat and want more insight into how to make their bond deeper and more meaningful. It's for these people that I've written *Mrs. Allen:* On All Fours.

This isn't a training book, although you will find training

tips and suggestions throughout. It's more of a manual for how to live happily with your pet — how to make him a part of your daily life so that both of you can benefit. Use the work book section to record your own observations and experiences with your pet. With a little work and a lot of love and attention, pets can be some of our best friends. I hope that this book helps you and your pet develop a perfect relationship — one that brings both of you much joy.

Barbara Allen

1

Developing the Perfect Relationship

The way I see it, there's no such thing as a perfect animal. Just like people, dogs, cats, and other critters slip up and make mistakes. You can't make an animal perfect — but you can work on making your relationship with that animal perfect.

What do I mean by a perfect pet relationship? To me, it's a relationship in which that pet has a special place within the family. My German Shepherd, Jano, goes everywhere with us —

Jano is my shadow at home and at work

he's literally with me 24 hours a day. I can trust him around my two young daughters, I can trust him around clients and guests, and I can trust him with strangers.

By trust, I mean that I know Jano will behave appropriately in a given situation. My five-year old daughter, Chandler, can step over him or hug him vigorously, and he'll respond in a gentle manner. When a guest visits my home or office, he may walk out to greet them, or notify me of their presence with a quiet "woof"! A stranger's presence at the door is announced with more authority.

Jano didn't learn how to behave in these different situations overnight. It took time on my part and lots of hard work for both of us. But to me, that time and work is part of the pleasure of owning a pet. I've never understood the purpose of keeping a dog tied up in the backyard, or having a cat who was aloof and preferred to be left alone. With that level of interaction, why not just have a goldfish?

I've been around animals of all kinds for most of my life, I've had the luxury of working with some of the best trainers in the country, and I can tell you that you get out of your pet's life what you put into it. If you are content to have a pet that simply looks nice, and whose interaction with you is confined to feeding it twice a day, that's fine. But if you want a deeper, more meaningful relationship, which I believe most pet owners do, I'd like to offer some suggestions that can help. Although every pet may have his own personality, and there may be differences in your particular situation, I've used these techniques on everything from purebred cats to rescue puppies, and they have almost always worked for me.

Pick pets carefully. The animal that you bring home will live with you and your family for 10 years or more, if all goes well. That's a long time to spend together. In addition, even the cheapest pet costs money — there are vaccinations, medications, pet food, and equipment to purchase, plus the cost of the animal itself.

When you add up the investment you'll be making in time and money, it makes sense to put some thought into the type of pet you want. What type of lifestyle do you live? How do you expect the pet to fit in? Are you looking for an active animal that you can take jogging or hiking, or a pet that's more of a couch potato? Would you enjoy spending hours each week grooming and brushing, or would you prefer a pet that just needs a few minutes of care each day? Is your ideal pet large, small, or medium-sized?

When you know what characteristics, both physical and mental, you are looking for, read some breed books, and talk with breeders and other pet owners. Ask about habits their dogs might have that aren't covered in the books. Before you fall in love with a breed, try to see a live representation of it, not just photos in a magazine.

Breed shows can be a great place to meet pets and their owners and get more information. So can obedience and agility shows, lure coursing trials, and other types of activities. For

Children and puppies can be great companions if both are properly trained and supervised.

17

information on when these shows are held, check the back of pet magazines, ask your vet, or look in the events section of your local newspaper.

In addition to what kind of pet you'd like, spend some time thinking about where to find it. Reputable breeders can be an excellent choice. Look for someone who belongs to his or her breed club — although not a solid endorsement, it usually shows that the person is serious about the welfare of the breed. Likewise, it's always good if the breeder is involved in rescue activities — if he or she won't help others with problem puppies or kittens, what guarantee do you have that you'll get help with yours? The breeder should also stand behind his or her "babies" — guaranteeing them from major health problems, and requesting that, should problems develop, the pet be returned.

Animal shelters or rescue groups can also be great places to find a pet. Although with mixed breed animals, you may not be able to determine much about their history or size, a knowledgeable rescue worker should be able to give you some idea of the animal's temperament, eventual size, and likes and dislikes. Plus, you have the added bonus of helping an animal in need. Over the years, I've rescued numerous dogs and cats from shelters or bad situations, and with them developed some of my most rewarding relationships.

Puppy or dog, kitten or cat? There's something irresistible about a puppy or kitten. The fuzzy coat, wide eyes, and wrinkled forehead are absolutely adorable, as is the wonder with which they encounter everything from shoes to soap bubbles.

But that same enchanting innocence that wins your heart can also drive you crazy, particularly when your new friend has kept you up for the third night in a row, yowling about everything and nothing in particular. For some people, puppies, kittens, and the major work they require just isn't worth it. For them, an adult pet may be a better choice.

In most cases, it's likely that the adult pet is already house

Puppies and kittens are cute, but require a lot of time and patience.

broken, and may have at least a rudimentary understanding of basic obedience. In addition, you know exactly what size the dog or cat will be, because he's already reached it. Finally, many adult pets are so grateful to be given a second chance at a family that I honestly believe they repay their new owners with double doses of loyalty and affection.

If you would like to adopt an adult pet, talk with your local shelter or the rescue coordinator for the breed in which you are interested. Whenever possible, find out if the animal in question has been temperament tested, what his history is, and what, if any, problems he may have. Once you have the full picture, you'll have a better idea if this animal is for you.

Set the rules from the start. Before your new pet comes home, think about what you expect of him. At my house, the basic rules include:

- no animals on the furniture/kitchen counters

- no needless noise (barking is allowed only when there's a knock on the door)
- no jumping on people
- no fighting
- 100 percent tolerance of children.

All of our pets — dogs and cats — MUST follow these rules. We also have other rules that aren't as serious. For example, we've taught all of the dogs to wipe their faces on the mat after they take a drink of water, to reduce dripping.

Your house may have different needs and different rules. My point is that you should decide what type of behavior you expect before your pet comes home, not after. Then you should discuss those rules with everyone in your family to make sure you all agree. If one rule is "No begging from the table," but your son insists on feeding your dog bits of his dinner, you are setting the dog up for failure. If you've taught your cat to stay off the couch, but your daughter lets her sneak up whenever you're away from home, you aren't being fair to the animal. For the rules to work, everyone — both pets and people — needs to know what is expected.

That brings me to another point. Pets aren't born knowing instinctively what's right and what's wrong. Most truly want to please you, but they have to be taught how to do that. Whacking a puppy on the rump or head the first time he puts a paw on the couch isn't teaching him to stay off the furniture — it's teaching him to move out of your way whenever you have a newspaper in your hand. Before you can enforce the rules, you have to make sure your pet understands them. That leads to yet another point:

Invest in a crate. Pet owners who have never used crates before look aghast when I suggest one, particularly if their pet is a cat. But crates, in addition to being a safe, secure place, can be wonderful training tools.

If you've ever had a toddler in your house, try to recall how you interacted with her. Did you leave her alone in the room while you were watching television, talking on the phone, or reading a book? I doubt it. You probably let her explore the room under your strict supervision. You took her hands off of any breakables that were left out, kept her from knocking over

Rescuing a mature dog or cat is another way to become a pet owner.

21

the lamp, and made sure she didn't stick her fingers in the hinges of the door. When you couldn't give the baby your full attention, you put her in her crib or playpen.

Most people would never dream of giving a toddler complete access to their house, but they think nothing of letting a puppy or kitten roam unsupervised. And then they act surprised when the animal has an accident, chews on a favorite slipper, or scratches the leather couch. And they blame the animal for something that is their own fault.

Just like that toddler, the pet doesn't yet know the rules. The only way he can learn is if someone takes the time to show him. The best way to do this is to let the pet explore under your supervision. Redirect his attention when he's doing something he's not supposed to. Show him what is acceptable. And when you can't supervise him, put him in his crate. It's the equivalent of your baby's playpen — a nice, safe place from which he can watch the world.

A crate shouldn't be a prison. It should be large enough to turn around in, but cozy enough for the animal to feel secure. Add a few toys, but stay away from soft bedding until he's housebroken. Take him out every hour or so to relieve himself, to play with you, and to explore. When you can't give him your full attention, back he goes in the crate. If you follow this routine, I guarantee that your pet will be housebroken in a minimal amount of time, and that damage to your belongings will be nonexistent.

Keep pets close. One technique I've just started to use is an old trainer's trick. Get a six-foot long web leash. Whenever your pet is outside of the crate, attach one end to your belt and the other to his collar. Wherever you go, your pet goes, and vice versa. It works well for two reasons: It's hard not to pay attention to a squirming, wriggling puppy or kitten on the end of the leash. It will keep you focused on what your pet is doing. Conversely, it will also keep your pet focused on you. He'll get used to moving with you as the center of his universe, which will be great when you start off-leash training.

Communication goes both ways. Before I try to teach a new pet anything, I spend some serious time learning how he communicates with me. To teach someone how to speak a different language, it helps if you know their own.

I don't mean barking or yowling. I am referring to the signals and cues my animals give that indicate their wants, dislikes, and needs. What does a new puppy do right before he pees? Does he sniff the ground, turn in circles, or paw at a spot? How does a kitten indicate that she's hungry? By yowling, rubbing against my legs, or scratching at the cabinet?

For the first few days of an animal's life with me, I spend some serious time just studying him. I take notes and observe the animal in different situations. Once I have established what signals the pet uses, I can build on that information.

For example, if a puppy always sniffs just before he eliminates, that's my cue to get him outside as fast as possible. He's teaching me his signal for when he has to go: I'm showing him the correct place in which to do it. By paying attention to his signals, I'm making it harder for him to make a mistake. Later, I can build on this by teaching him to eliminate on command: Just as he squats to pee, I'll tell him "Hurry up." Eventually, he'll associate the word with the act — a great command for those days when it's cold, windy, and he's taking his time finding the correct spot.

Obedience training is for everyone. Whenever someone I know gets a new pet, I always ask when they will be starting obedience classes. "Oh, Spike doesn't need those — he's just a pet," is the standard reply. And I always tell them that that's all the more reason to go to class.

Obedience training can do wonderful things for your pet. It can firmly establish you as being in charge of the relationship, which is what you want. It also teaches the basic good manners that your pet will need to be welcome anywhere. It gives your pet a chance to use his brain in a positive way. Finally, the work that you do together will create a strong bond between you.

I'm a firm believer in positive training. It's not that my pets don't receive corrections — they do. But the emphasis is on rewarding the right behavior, not punishing the wrong one. I've trained with numerous people over the years, and I know what type of training makes me feel comfortable. I don't let other people — even trainers — correct my dogs. I look for a trainer who runs the class in a business-like, professional manner; who answers my questions willingly; and who treats my dog in a respectful manner.

You may have different criteria for a trainer. Whatever you are looking for, keep searching until you find someone who will work with you and your pet, and teach you both how to communicate with each other and build the best relationship possible. You owe your pet — and yourself — nothing less.

Try It Yourself

Equipment for building a great relationship:

- a crate or carrier

- long leash

- time

- patience

Questions to ask:

What type of pet will fit into my life?

What type of a relationship do I want to have with him?

What am I willing to do to develop that relationship?

What rules must my pet follow? Do you expect your new pet to stay off the furniture, behave around children, not jump up, etc.?

How will I communicate these rules to him?

Top 10 Tips

1. **Your relationship with your pet is like a bank account.** You can only take out of it what you put into it. The more time and energy you spend on your pet, the more you will be rewarded.

2. **Pick pets carefully.** If all goes well, your pet will live with you for 10 or more years — longer than you'll keep your current car. A few hours of homework can help ensure that those years will be pleasant, enjoyable ones for both you and your pet.

3. **Puppy or dog, kitten or cat?** Baby animals are cute, but not everyone has the time and patience to train them. Adopting a mature animal can be a great alternative.

4. **Set the rules from the start.** Behavior that's cute in a 10-pound puppy can be dangerous in a 100-pound adult. If you don't want your pet jumping on people, begging from the table, or sleeping on the furniture as an adult, don't let him do it as a baby.

5. **Invest in a crate.** Crates aren't prisons if they are used correctly — they are safe, comfortable rooms that dogs and cats can call their own. Crates can help reduce accidents and speed up housebreaking, too.

6. **Keep pets close.** You wouldn't let a toddler wander around your house unsupervised — new pets need to be overseen in the same way.

7. **Communication goes both ways.** You can't expect to teach your pet what you want if you don't speak his language. Spend the first few days watching him settle in, and learn to read his signals about food, bathroom breaks, and sleep.

8. **Obedience training is for everyone.** Whether your pet is a purebred or a mixed-breed, he needs to know how to behave. Teach him a few simple commands and he'll be welcome anywhere.

9. **Keep it positive.** Obedience-training should be an enjoyable way for you and your pet to spend time together — not something to dread.

10. **Find a trainer you can trust.** A good obedience trainer can help you establish a warm bond with your pet. Look for someone who treats your pet as an individual, listens to your goals and concerns, and uses methods with which you feel comfortable.

2

Communication Is Key

Think of any good relationship — that between a parent and child, husband and wife, friend and friend. When you list the characteristics that make the relationship a positive one, what comes to mind? It's likely that communication is at the top of the list. If two people can't communicate well with each other, it's difficult to develop a constructive relationship.

Relationships with pets are the same way. To build a positive union with your pet, you need to be able to communicate with him. But like any good relationship, communication with pets is a two-way street. Many people think that because animals can't talk, they can't communicate, and that the owner's only role is to give orders and make sure they are obeyed. That's simply not true.

As a pet owner, you have a double responsibility when it comes to communication; to make sure that your pet understands you, and to make sure that you understand your pet. It's like being in charge of negotiations with someone who doesn't speak the same language. Not only do you need to make sure your point gets across, but you also have to take care that your companion's view is expressed as well.

Good communication can help you train better, recognize when your pet is ill, and build a positive, long-lasting relationship. Ultimately, any breakdowns in communication are your responsibility, not your pet's. If the dialogue between the two of you isn't going well, you need to figure out why and how to change it.

Obviously, pet's don't "talk" in the way we do. But if you

have patience and pay attention, you can figure out what is going on. Your pet's body language, the pitch of his bark or meow, the way he looks at you, the speed with which he responds to a command, can all tell you something — you just need to watch and listen.

The following are tips that I've learned after years of working with trainers, researching the subject, and spending time with my own animals. I hope they are helpful in opening up a dialogue with your pet.

Send the right message from the very beginning. The way you communicate with your pet from the first day will have a big impact on your relationship when he's a grown dog or cat. Think hard about what you want to say before you bring him home.

For example, New York trainer Deb Zappia notes that there is a big difference between the way you'd treat a puppy destined to be a house pet, and one that you want to train for competition. To keep a future competition candidate enthusiastic, Zappia allows behavior, such as running, body-slamming, and rough play, that she wouldn't allow in a pet. "Once you take that enthusiasm and drive out, you may never get it back," she said.

On the other hand, a pet puppy may not need that level of enthusiasm and drive to compete, so Zappia works to extinguish behaviors that typical pet owners have a hard time living with, such as jumping up.

That's not to say a pet destined for obedience or other competition can't be a good house pet too, according to Zappia. It just may take more time to train him. Zappia points to my German Shepherd Dog, Jano, as a perfect example.

As a puppy, Jano was very energetic. He'd run to get his toys, body slam into people, and generally act like a wild child. He was allowed to keep those behaviors until he was about two years old, when his more formal training began. Today, Jano is

*Deb Zappia, a top New York trainer, works hard to develop a
strong rapport with the animals she trains.*

extremely calm, very bonded with me, and yet is still capable of going out on a competitive obedience course and bringing home top scores. Training him this way took more work, but to me it was worth it.

To communicate what's acceptable and what's not to your pet, you need to think about your goals for him. The time to do this isn't when your puppy is leaping over the sofa, or your kitten is sitting on the counter — it's before the animal ever comes to live with you.

The medium is as important as the message. Zappia sees owners all the time who purchase breeds destined to be big, strong adult animals. In an effort to start controlling them as puppies, they start flipping the animals onto their backs into a submissive pose, handling them roughly, or trying to intimidate them into good behavior.

The problem is that those cute, 15 pound puppies can grow up into 100 pound animals with strong wills. Bullying a dog of this size is a different story. "The animal grows up, and they have no relationship except one built on adversity," she said.

The better, safer approach to sending the signal that you are in charge is to try to build a rapport with your pet from a young age. Spend time doing things that your pet considers fun — playing catch, taking walks, chasing toys — and you'll build a relationship built on trust. From there, you can work with a trainer to establish your control in a positive way.

Be consistent. One of the biggest problems Zappia encounters with animal owners is a lack of consistency. Owners may give their pet a command and not enforce it three or four times, then correct the pet with a vengeance for not listening the fifth time. Or, they may allow certain behaviors on one day, and not allow them the next.

To teach your pet what you mean, you need to make sure that you are saying the same thing every time. How quickly would you learn a foreign language if every time your teacher said a word, she changed the meaning? Teaching your pet is the same.

My rule at home is "one command, one action." I always use the same word for a command. Once my pets know a command, I expect them to respond to it the first time I give it. If you tell your dog or cat "off," for example, and wait until the third time you say it for them to respond, what you are telling them is that your first two commands can be ignored. Your pet needs to be able to trust that you mean what you say — being inconsistent with your commands does the exact opposite.

Watch what you say — and how you say it. Animals are often smarter than we give them credit for. They can recognize not only words, but tone of voice, often better than many people can. If you are angry and upset when giving a command to your pet, it's likely that he will sense it. Even if your anger isn't directed at him, his head may droop, his ears may go back, and he may hold his tail between his legs.

If you've had a bad day at the office, or if you are frustrated with your family, hold off on working with your pet. You want time spent with you to be a positive experience, and if your animal believes you are angry with him — even if that's erroneous — he won't enjoy the session. Instead, do something fun that will relieve your anger and that won't put any pressure to perform on your pet. Take a walk, throw a ball, or play with a favorite toy.

Keep in mind, too, that pets may recognize certain words outside of conversations with you. Stephen O'Donnell, a K-9 officer with the Hartford, CT police department, knew a dog who recognized his unit's number. When it would come over the radio, he'd perk up his ears and get closer, as if trying to figure out where he and his partner would be sent. Other pet owners talk about having to spell the word "car" or "trip" to avoid having their animal go into a frenzy of excitement.

K-9 Officer Stephen O'Donnell's safety often depends on how well he can read his four-footed partner's signals.

Frequently, dogs and cats also recognize their names. If you are talking about your pet, try to avoid using his name in front of him. His name should be primarily associated with directions from you — if you bandy it about, he may stop paying attention to it.

Quantity time results in quality communications. Have you ever been around two people who have been friends for a long time? They may finish each other's sentences, use the same words to describe something, or appear to be reading each other's minds. It's not that they have some mysterious powers — it's simply that they've spent lots of time together. They know how and what the other person is trying to communicate based on past experience.

"I see dogs and owners all the time who don't have a working relationship built on trust and friendship. They're not connected," Zappia said. Pets aren't accessories that can be taken out of a closet when convenient, and then put away for days at a time. They are living creatures that have a strong need to be a part of their owners' lives.

"Everybody has to work today," she said. "But you can't leave a puppy home alone for 15 hours a day, seven days a week." The result will be an animal with explosive energy. When new owners are greeted by wild running and jumping, they often become angry and put the animal back in its crate, which just exacerbates the problem.

Police officer O'Donnell is one of the lucky pet owners. As a K-9 officer, his dog lives and works with him. His first partner, a German Shepherd Dog named Kitt, was with him for seven years.

O'Donnell's safety often depends on being able to understand what his dog is telling him. "You've got to rely on your dog," he said. Because O'Donnell and Kitt spent so much time together, O'Donnell was able to read the smallest signal from Kitt, such as what it meant when Kitt held his tail to the left as opposed to the right when tracking. But getting to this point took a good two years, he said.

Not everyone can be as fortunate as O'Donnell. But you can still make an effort to spend as much time as possible with your pet. Take your pet for walks and hikes on the weekend. During the week, make a point to include him on short errands. Many stores will allow well-behaved animals inside (just watch out for damage done by wagging tails!). When you are visiting friends, ask if your pet is welcome.

Seeing your pet in different situations will improve your ability to communicate with him, because he'll be faced with different stimuli than he would be at home, exposing you to a wider range of his reactions and signals.

Remember your pet is an individual. When training, Zappia takes into account not only an animal's breed, but his or her individual drives, desires, and responses. She and the owner work together to read what the animal is telling them regarding the training he is receiving — how well he tolerates a correction, what exercises he enjoys, what drills he doesn't — to devise the best program for his particular needs.

O'Donnell, too, needs to remember that animals are individuals. When his first dog Kitt died of cancer at the age of ten, my company Stabar helped him to find, train, and purchase a new partner. Jake is a beautiful, two year old German Shepherd male who is learning the ropes on the streets of Hartford. O'Donnell, meanwhile, is still learning to read what his new partner's posture, body language, and movement means.

"They tell you to never compare your new dog to your old one, and I try not to," O'Donnell said. Instead, he's concentrating on discovering Jake's strengths, building up his weak areas, and learning to communicate with him.

"It takes work and persistence," he said. O'Donnell points to times that he's missed suspects when tracking because he'd second-guessed the dog. "The cops who are there will tell you the subject went left, but the dog wants to go right. You correct the dog because you think that the dog can't be smarter than the person. Later, the subject may be found off to the right, where the dog wanted to go all along."

"You've got to learn to trust the dog," O'Donnell said.

Consciously try to read your pet's cues. Invest in an animal behavior book, or simply take notes on what your pet does to alert you to a desire or need. Does your cat start to yowl every evening around the same time? Run through a list of items that might satisfy her. If you offer her food and she accepts, it might be her signal for telling you she's hungry. If not, try a toy — it could be that she's bored and seeking your attention.

One family I know has a generally well-behaved dog. When the couple sits down to watch television at night, however, the dog will run to the woman's closet, open it, and extract a shoe. He knows that chewing on items that aren't his is forbidden, so he'll gently carry the shoe into the living room and drop it just out of the couple's reach. It's a play for their attention.

O'Donnell generally works the 2 p.m. to 10:30 p.m. shift in Hartford. Somewhere around 5, Jake gets restless, whines, and paces in the back of the car. O'Donnell has finally realized that Jake needs a regular "bathroom break" at this time, and his pacing and other behaviors have been an attempt to signal this.

Pets have their own communication skills — we just need to pay attention to figure them out. A puppy who crouches, tail waving above his back, body wriggling, is signaling his invitation to play. A cat who's tail switches back and forth in a quick, jerky manner may be excited or irritated. A dog who rolls onto his back and piddles is signaling his submission to you. A cat who jumps into your lap, curls up, and begins kneading is contented.

It's your job to read these signals and respond correctly to them. Punishing a dog for piddling in the above example is pointless — he's already doing everything he can to show you he wants to please, and is asking you not to hurt him. A better approach would be to pay no attention to the behavior, or calmly make yourself as nonthreatening as possible. Avoid standing over the dog, which can be intimidating. Instead, sit on the floor a short distance away. Try to avoid direct eye contact, which can be threatening to some animals. Let the dog come to you, and pet it when it stands upright and does not urinate submissively.

Communicating with your pet takes work on your part. "People don't realize how much time goes into a dog," said O'Donnell, and the same could be said of cats. But the time you spend learning to communicate effectively with your pet will pay off in a solid relationship built on trust and understanding.

Champion horse trainer Carl Dascole says communication is the key to successfully training any animal.

| *Try It Yourself* |

Questions to ask:

Learning to communicate well with your pet takes time. The first thing I do when I bring a new animal home is spend a few days just observing it. Doing so can tell you a lot about its signals. Even if you've had your pet for a long time, take a few days to watch him closely. Ask yourself the following questions, and record your answers in the space below:

What does your pet do just before it defecates? Does it sniff, circle, squat, or paw the soil in front of it? These clues are your pet's way of telling you he has to go. Pay attention to them, and housebreaking will be a breeze.

How does your pet signal his hunger? Does he whine, bark, meow, or rub against your legs?

How does your pet indicate that he wants to play? Does he paw at you, run in circles, crouch on his front legs with his rump in the air, or pounce?

How do you know when your pet is afraid or uncomfortable? Does he whine, try to retreat, hold his body in a rigid position, or overcompensate by acting in an aggressive manner?

You may be surprised by some of the answers. Knowing what your pet is trying to tell you can go a long way toward improving your ability to communicate with him. It can also help you head off dangerous situations, such as a dog or cat fight, by recognizing your pet's signals before he takes action.

Top 10 Tips

1. **Communication is a two-way street.** It's true that your pet needs to listen to you, but to get the most out of the relationship, you must be able to understand your pet as well.

2. **Send the right message from the beginning.** How you relate to your pet on the first day can have long-lasting implications for your relationship. If you start out as a pushover, it's going to be hard to convince your dog or cat that you mean business later on. On the other hand, coming across as a drill sergeant won't win you points either.

3. **Think about your goals.** Before you can decide how to communicate with your pet, you need to determine what you want from the relationship. Do you expect competition-level attention and obedience, or a laid-back couch potato?

4. **The medium is as important as the message.** A loud voice and a hand that's quick to correct may get you obedience — but it probably won't get you a pet that's eager to be around you.

5. **Be consistent.** If you drag your pet off the couch one day, then let him stay on the next, you're sending a confusing message. The rules and the words you use to convey them should stay the same at all times.

6. **Watch what you say — and how you say it.** Don't train when you are angry, and avoid using your pet's name or common commands around him unless you expect action.

7. **Quantity time results in quality communications.** To develop an intuitive ability to communicate with your pet takes time — lots of it. You need to know how your pet responds in different situations, with different people, under different conditions. All of this takes time.

8. **Remember your pet is an individual.** What works to get and hold the attention of your pet is different from what another animal needs. As owner, it's up to you to figure out your pet's personality and work with it.

9. **Consciously try to read your pet's cues.** Watch him, read a book on animal behavior, or work with a good trainer. Figure out what he's trying to tell you.

10. **Communicating with pets takes hard work.** It's not something that will happen overnight. But the results are worth it.

3

Genetics = Purpose and Potential

Misty was a three-year-old herding dog, with an outgoing personality and enough energy to power a small city. Her first owners turned her in because she was just too much for them to handle. Her second owners fell in love with her good looks and took her home. Although the shelter worker who placed Misty advised lots of exercise and obedience work, the couple did neither. After all, they reasoned, she wasn't a "show dog," and so didn't need to be in peak condition, or be able to do fancy tricks.

With no way to positively channel her energy, Misty turned destructive; she barked, chased people and cars, and growled at her owners when they reprimanded her. Eventually, the growling turned to nipping, and then biting. Two months after she was adopted, Misty was put down.

I'm involved in a lot of rescue work, both through my company and in my private life. To me, there's nothing

Dogs that are bred to work may become frustrated if their talents aren't used.

43

Don't purchase a pet on looks alone. Learn about the breed's history, temperament, and health before making a decision.

sadder than seeing a dog or cat discarded or put down because its owners didn't have the time, energy, or knowledge to deal with it. It's true that there are some animals that just don't make good pets, either through temperament or physical problems. But I believe that those types of dogs and cats are few and far between. A little research about the type of pet you are adopting can help you determine how well that animal will fit into your life.

With enough exercise and work, Misty would have made a wonderful pet. Her owners made several mistakes that could easily have been avoided with a little effort on their part. To begin with, they never properly researched her breed. If they had, they would have known that they were adopting a smart dog, meant for serious work. They ignored the advice of the rescue worker, and they let a dog known to be dominant try to run their lives. The result was disaster, and Misty was the one who paid for their ignorance — with her life.

On the other hand, I have seen some success stories. Mary was a woman in her seventies who had trained and competed with dogs all of her life. She wanted a smart dog, who would be able to learn quickly, and she wanted an animal that was relatively small. Rex was an abused dog who, when he was rescued, was frozen to the ground. He'd been tied in the backyard for most of his young life, and had never seen another dog. He hated everyone, tried to fight with every dog he saw, and almost killed several cats.

Mary spent an incredible amount of time and effort rehabilitating Rex, and two years later he competed in obedience, obtaining several titles. The breed traits that were a liability for Rex's first owner — his sharpness and energy — were assets in his relationship with Mary.

To make sure you get the pet that's right for you, it's important to do your homework up-front. Here are some suggestions to consider:

Be honest about what you want. Whether it's a cat, a dog, or a goldfish, pet ownership takes work. For many people, that work — feeding, grooming, and training — is what a relationship with an animal is all about. For other people, it's simply an unwanted hassle and responsibility. That's fine too. Not everyone needs to own an animal to be happy, but if it's not something you desire, be honest. If you are the primary care giver in your family, don't let anyone pressure you into getting an animal you don't want. You — and the pet — will both end up unhappy.

Consider your lifestyle. What do you want from a pet? Someone to run with, or someone to curl up on the couch with you at night? Do you have enough time to spend training a puppy or kitten, or would you be better off with an older animal that requires less work? Are you looking for an agreeable, laid-back pet, or one with a mind of its own that will make training more of a challenge?

Also take into consideration your surroundings. Although big dogs can be kept in small apartments, know that if you love the look of a Mastiff, there are drawbacks that come along with that size. How will you transport a large pet? What if you have children — can you fit them and the dog in your car? When considering an animal, remember that pet ownership is an investment that can last for 10 or more years. You need to look not just at your lifestyle today, but at what you anticipate it will be down the road.

Purebred or rescue? Lots of people have never paid for a pet; they've adopted them from shelters, or been given a kitten or puppy when their neighbor's animal had a litter. They don't see the point of paying for something they can get for free. "Who needs a bunch of papers?" is a common comment. "My dog/cat is as good as any fancy show pet."

Rescue animals can make wonderful pets, but it's important to learn as much about the animal as possible before adopting it.

The point is a valid one. Adopting a dog or cat from the local shelter is a great way to find a wonderful pet that needs a home. What most mixed breeds can't provide, however, is a guarantee of how they will turn out. Breeders can't provide a guarantee, either, but if they are using a responsible breeding program, they should have a pretty good idea of the future size, weight, and characteristics of the ball of fluff you've fallen in love with. They can show you the parents, so that you know what the adult dog or cat may look like, and they can tell you how they guard against defects common to the breed. Good breeders will also be there to guide you through your pet's adolescence, which can be a trying time, and to help you with any problems you encounter.

Either choice, mix or purebred, can be a good one. It all depends on what you want from your pet, and what you hope to do with him or her.

Do your homework. There's a cat or dog for almost any situation. Some breeds bark or meow, some don't. Some have a high energy drive, others prefer to spend most of the day quietly napping. Some are known for being whip-smart; others have a good-natured reputation but are not the brightest bulb in the factory. Before you purchase a pet, know what characteristics the breed is supposed to have. If you love the look of herding dogs, but are afraid they'll constantly be rounding up your children, for example, you may want to reconsider your choice, or at least speak with a breeder about your concerns.

Good sources to research include breed books, particularly those that are devoted to a single breed of dog or cat. Most breeds have their own clubs, which you can contact through the AKC, or by searching for them on the internet. Clubs may in turn lead you to breeders willing to spend some time educating you on the quirks of their breed.

Attending a dog or cat show is another good way to get more information about the breeds or breed in which you are interested. Attending a show will also give you a good look, up close, at how youngsters and adult representatives of your chosen breed should look and act. Does the animal resemble the breed in your books? Is it larger or smaller? More outgoing, or more reserved than you expected it to be? Don't just talk with one breeder at a show. Try to speak with several, and observe their animals to get a sense of differences within the breed.

Genetics aren't everything. I honestly believe that there are larger differences between individual dogs or cats of the same breed than between different breeds. In my opinion, good, consistent training can overcome almost anything. There are of course exceptions; some dog breeds bred for fighting, for example, may never overcome this desire when they are around other animals. But in general, a dog or cat that's come from a solid environment and has been trained in the essentials —

That cute ball of fluff can grow quickly, so make sure you're prepared to deal with the adult version of the pet you decide to bring home.

housebreaking, good manners, and basic obedience — can be happy in almost any situation.

Friends of mine own two Rhodesian Ridgebacks. Every time they showed up at a different event, such as agility or obedience, they'd hear the same refrain: "Ridgebacks can't do this." The owners didn't know that Ridgebacks in general weren't supposed to be good at certain activities. What they knew was that they wanted their dogs to try it, so they did.

There are experts who will tell you that this or that breed of dog or cat is great with children. Other experts will turn around and tell you the exact opposite about the same breed. I'd rather make my decision based on observation of a particular dog or cat, his parents, and his environment. Although genetics can give you some indication of what you are purchasing, every animal is different.

When you've narrowed down your search to a single breed, don't buy from the first breeder you encounter. Talk with several. Ask them what traits their animals are known for, and what they are trying to accomplish with their breeding program. Is their goal an animal that's sound in mind and body and meets their breed standard? Do they breed working stock — pets that are used for the purpose they were originally intended for, such as herding or hunting — or do they breed primarily for appearance? Any reputable breeder should be able and willing to answer these types of questions.

If you are serious about purchasing from a particular breeder, ask to see the animal's parents. At least one of them should be on the property. Are they healthy looking, alert, and vibrant? Friendly or cowed? Females who have recently given birth may not be in the best condition, and may be guarded around their babies, but should still look sound. Do the parents act and look the way you envision your pet as an adult?

For mixed breed or rescue animals, this type of research can be more difficult. Try to get a sense from the shelter worker of what the animal's former life was like, what breeds may have played a part in its background, and any other information you can glean. Only when you've done as much research as possible should you commit to taking a particular pet home.

Prepare for potential problems. Almost every breed of cat or dog has specific ailments that are common to the breed and type of animal. Deafness, hip problems, and vision impairment are just a few of the more common issues pet owners encounter. If you've done your homework during the research stage, you'll know what to expect. Armed with that knowledge, talk with your breeder about the appearance of these traits in his or her stock. How often does it show up? What steps does the breeder take to safeguard against it? What tests has he or she performed on your potential pet's parents, such as x-raying hips and elbows for dysplasia? Ask to see a copy of the results — don't take the breeder's word on faith alone.

What happens if the problem shows up in your pet? What guarantees does the breeder make? Some will pay a portion of the treatment costs, if treatment is an option. Others will refund the purchase price of the animal. Still others will exchange the pet for another one. Think about what you are comfortable with before you commit. After it has spent a few days in your house, you may not be able to imagine giving back that cuddly puppy or kitten and making room in your heart for a replacement.

Utilize your breed's skills and abilities. If your dog or cat is known for doing something well, why not take advantage of it? Herding can show off the talents of Border Collies or Australian Shepherds. Retrievers may thrive on field trials. And the activity doesn't have to be a competitive one — if your Siamese is good at "talking," encourage her. Let your pet's breed strengths shine through, and he'll be a more confident, secure animal. Plus, by channeling the behavior in a positive way, you'll have a pet that's easier to live with.

Take training seriously. At the risk of repeating myself, I'm going to say it again — good training is the key to a successful, happy relationship with any pet. Dog or cat, big or small, all pets should have at least a rudimentary introduction to training — housebreaking, manners, and basic obedience.

Some large, powerful dogs, bred to be aggressive, may require more work than others. But just because you've chosen a small, lap-sized dog doesn't mean you can skimp on training. I've seen it time and time again — small pets bark inappropriately, or growl, or jump, or paw at people, and it's dismissed as "cute." Their owners would be horrified if a large dog acted the same way. No matter what size or type pet you have, good manners are good manners, and teaching them is an essential part of the pet/owner relationship.

Even the best breeding program can't give you the perfect pet. Only you, through time and training, can accomplish that.

> ## *Try It Yourself*

Places to research breeds:

- breed clubs and societies

- the internet

- local shows

- breed books and standards

Questions that can help you decide on a breed:

What do I want from this pet? Do you want to show it in conformation, obedience, or agility? Would you like a pet that enjoys retrieving or playing frisbee? Do you want an easy-going companion, or an energetic pet who can go hiking or running with you? Do you prefer laid-back animals, or those that are more of a challenge?

What is my lifestyle like? Are you active, or sedentary? Do you have a yard? Do you have children? Do you live in a hot climate or a more temperate zone? Do you have the time and energy to train a puppy or kitten? Do you travel frequently?

What look do I like in a pet? Some pet owners can't conceive of a cat or dog without a full, fluffy coat. Others prefer a more stream-lined look. It makes sense to purchase a pet based on a look that appeals to you, if you've done the surrounding home-work and are comfortable with the other traits the breed has.

How much time am I willing to spend on grooming and care? All animals require some level of grooming. My food supplement SHED-STOP can eliminate year-round shedding, but dogs and cats still need to shed seasonally. How do you feel about having long hairs draped over furniture or clothing? Are you willing to spend the time detangling knots in a heavy coat? If you aren't, can you afford to pay someone to do it?

What are the training requirements of the breed? If you are in love with a big, aggressive breed of dog, you'd better be prepared to put the time and effort into training and socializing your pet from the beginning. What's cute in a 40 pound puppy can be downright dangerous in an adult dog. Some small breeds can be difficult to train as well. Talk with local obedience instructors about tendencies they've noticed in these breeds, and get a breeder's input too.

Top 10 Tips

1. **Be honest about what you want.** Owning a dog or cat isn't for everyone. Don't talk yourself into a responsibility you don't want, and don't let anyone else talk you into it either.

2. **Consider your lifestyle.** Your living space, activity level, and tolerance for chores such as grooming and exercising a pet can all influence which animal is best for you.

3. **Plan for the future.** Adopting a dog or cat is a long-term commitment. Will you still have the necessary time, space, and attention to give a pet in five or ten years?

4. **Purebred or rescue?** Either can be a great choice. A purebred pet from a reliable breeder isn't a guarantee, but does provide a better idea of what you'll wind up with two years from now. A rescue pet can be an inexpensive way to adopt a friend for life.

5. **Do your homework.** Research the traits and characteristics common to the breed in which you are interested. Read breed books, attend shows, and meet with breeders to get an idea of how the breed looks and acts.

6. **See the parents.** Once you've chosen a breed and breeder, whenever possible ask to meet your future pet's parents. If they are healthy, happy, and well-behaved, there's a good chance your pet will be too.

7. **Genetics aren't everything.** There can be bigger differences between individual animals than there are between breeds. Keep this in mind when pet-shopping.

8. **Prepare for potential problems.** Before your pet comes home, learn about defects that run in the breed, such as hip dysplasia or blindness. Discuss with your breeder what will happen if these problems appear in your pet — who will pay for vet bills? Will your purchase price be partially refunded? Get any guarantees in writing.

9. **Utilize your breed's skills and abilities.** Channel those talents into productive, fun activities.

10. **Take training seriously.** Purebred or mixed breed, dog or cat, makes no difference — training is the key to the perfect pet.

4

The Power of Positive Training

Jano, my German Shepherd Dog, goes everywhere with me — to work, to meetings, to pick up my daughters at school. Almost every day, a stranger will approach me and say "Your dog is so well-behaved. I wish my dog was like that." When I say "Well, why isn't he?" the person inevitably gives me a litany of excuses — the dog is too young, too old, too dumb, or they just don't have the know-how or time to train him.

Having a well-trained dog is like speaking French. You can't expect to become proficient overnight. It helps if you have a great instructor or book, but if you don't practice, you won't learn. If you stay with it and put enough time and energy in, eventually you'll stop parroting rote phrases and start creating your own.

Dog training is similar. Having a great instructor or book to guide you is important, but if you don't put the time in, you and your pet

Jano and I worked together for years to become a team.

will never get anywhere. If you do practice, once you master the basics, you'll be teaching him skills you may never have dreamed possible.

The other statement people make all the time when I discuss training is "Oh, I don't need some fancy training class for my dog. He's just a pet. He's never going to show." This drives me crazy. Pet dogs need training just as much, if not more, than show dogs. For many pets, a training class is their only exposure to other animals — important for socialization purposes. Training sessions allow you to set time aside and build a bond with your dog, a wonderful side-benefit of training. Finally, unlike some show dogs who live in kennels, most pets are an integral part of the family — they live inside, they are around children or elderly people, they regularly encounter mail carriers, delivery people, and other strangers. It's essential that they know how to respond appropriately in different situations. Only training can teach them that.

If you aren't training your pet, you are missing out on one of the best and most interesting aspects of the pet/owner relationship. When done correctly, training not only results in a well-behaved pet, but a pet that wants to be with you over anyone or anything else.

Although I'm not a trainer, I've had the luxury of working with some of the best in the business since the time I was fourteen. Here are some of the secrets I've learned — I hope you find them helpful.

Know your dog — and yourself. What do you want out of your pet? Are you expecting competition-level work, or are you happy with a dog that is reasonably well-behaved? Does your pet have the capability to do what you are asking of him, and are you willing to put the time and effort into getting there? What is his pain tolerance like? What motivates him? How comfortable are you giving commands and expecting them to be obeyed? Answering these questions honestly will go a long way toward determining the type and amount of training you do. There's an old training saying "You always get the dog you deserve." What type of dog do you deserve — and what are you willing to do to get it?

Most pets aren't prodigies. Trainer Richard Crane of New York doesn't believe in starting training sessions for dogs until they are mature enough to actually learn, usually around six months. Just as you wouldn't expect a child in kindergarten to master geometry, you shouldn't expect too much of your pet until this age.

Puppy classes can be useful if they are controlled and if socialization is positive, according to Crane. But up until six months, his puppies are taught only two things: to come when called, and to mind the house rules, such as staying off the

My pets go every-where with me — they even have their own crates at work!

furniture and out of the garbage.

"The problem is that you can't correct a puppy at that age. If you give a command and he chooses not to do it, he's learned that there are no consequences for negative behavior," Crane said. And since puppies don't have the attention span to master commands at this stage, you are setting him up for failure.

Find a good instructor. It's easier to train yourself and your dog if you've got someone with experience to guide you through the tricky spots. You should be comfortable with the person's methods, and be able to ask questions without feeling embarrassed. A good instructor will recognize that your pet is an individual, and that what works for someone else's dog may not work for yours. A good instructor will also ask you what your training goals are, help you to see if they are realistic, and then work with you to achieve them.

To find an instructor, talk with your veterinarian, with friends who have well-trained dogs, or with your breeder. Ask them to describe how the trainer they recommend works, and why they feel comfortable with him or her. Once you've narrowed down your choices, take the time to talk with each of the instructors you're considering. Doing this research at the beginning will save you and your pet time and aggravation later.

Master motivation. I'm a big believer in positive training. That's not to say I never correct my pets; I do. But I'd rather reward them than punish them, and I give them every possible opportunity when training to get a task right. Force rarely gives good results over the long term.

Before I start training a pet, I spend a lot of time just observing him to find out his likes and dislikes. Pets are like people in that they all like different things. One may have a strong food drive, another may love to play with a ball, and the third may be happiest getting a pat on the head and some praise. It's up to you to find out what pushes your pet's motivational buttons.

I find that using a variety of rewards and mixing them up can help hold my pet's interest during training. If he never knows what's coming next, he's more apt to pay attention, which is the whole point of successful training. I use rewards liberally during training, particularly during the learning stage. It's a way to make training more enjoyable for both the animal and me.

Training isn't just teaching — it's bonding with your pet. Would you rather spend time with someone who constantly yelled at you and/or whacked you on the head or rump, or with someone who spoke calmly, showed you what to do, and praised you

Corrections aren't bad, if they are done correctly.

when you did it right? The answer should be obvious.

Corrections aren't cruel — if they are done correctly.
There are lots of people who refuse to use corrections on their pet. That's their choice. There are other people who correct in a harsh or punitive manner. I don't consider either approach to be effective.

My philosophy is this: Once a pet has been truly taught a command, such as sit, he needs to know that there are negative consequences for not obeying. I'm not talking about the six-month-old puppy who has heard the word sit a few times, had his rump pushed down to make him do so, and then whacked with a newspaper the first time he doesn't obey. That's cruel.

But if your dog has been carefully, patiently, and consistently shown the meaning of the word sit, has sat on command numerous times, and then decides to blow you off the first time a good-looking French poodle comes around the corner, he needs to be taught that sit means just that, no matter what.

People always make excuses for their pet. They say things like "Oh, he usually listens — it's just that he's distracted by the food/dogs/cats." But think about it — what's the point of having a pet that just obeys when there are no distractions around? It's when there are interesting things going on that you most need to have your pet under control. And what's crueler — giving your pet a quick, effective correction, or letting him get hurt during a situation that could have been avoided if he'd obeyed you? Corrections, when done correctly, help your pet understand that obeying is not optional.

There's another reason to correct a disobedient dog. Training isn't just about commands — it's about creating a relationship. Although you and your pet become a team during the process, it's a team that must have a leader. Dogs are pack animals, and they are most comfortable when they know who's in charge. If you don't step up and assume that responsibility, your pet will.

At my house, I am unquestionably the pack leader. Our family tends to like large animals — Jano and Ace are German Shepherd Dogs, Sasha is a Bullmastiff, and Parker is an English Setter. If they didn't accept my leadership, I would have a difficult time controlling them. But because of the work we've put into training, and because they know that misbehavior is corrected, I can have 400 pounds of dog around the house.

Good training lets me have over 400 pounds of dog (and cat) around the house.

So, now that you know why corrections are important, how do you do them? A lot depends on the individual dog, and on your comfort level with giving corrections. One of my customers has a big mutt who is a cross between a couple of notoriously difficult breeds. Physically he's a rough, tough dog with a high pain tolerance. Mentally, he's a cupcake. A stern "bad dog," for serious offenses is much more effective than any physical correction could ever be.

On the other hand, there are dogs that respond to a physical remonstration. Some dogs really need to focus and know that you are serious, that obeying isn't optional, and a physical correction seems to be an effective way to reach them.

Richard Crane recommends using a prong or pinch collar over the more typically used choke collar, which can damage the soft tissue around the dog's throat if used incorrectly. Have your trainer demonstrate the correct way to put the collar on, and the right way to use it. The correction should be a quick, sharp tug that's a reality check, not a long, drawn out affair. The dog doesn't listen, the dog gets corrected, and Boom! you move on. Don't nag at the dog, or give a series of tentative tugs on the collar — that only reinforces his sense that you are not someone to take seriously. Time the correction to occur immediately after the incorrect behavior, so that the dog will associate the two actions together.

Crate training can eliminate most accidents, but just in case, I've developed an all-natural spot remover.

"But I don't want to hurt him, or get him mad at me," people always say. If you are doing it right, you won't. Crane is involved in the sport of Schutzhund, a three-part event that involves protection work, tracking, and obedience. "You lose points if the dog is not animated," he said. "Anyone can train a dog, but a dog that works in a correct and happy manner is well-trained." For Crane, corrections are an integral part of that training.

Be fair. Your pet needs to know that he can count on you. Once you've set the rules, you need to enforce them fairly. Don't use training sessions as a way to blow off steam — if you've had a bad day and are getting frustrated with your pet, end the training session before you do any damage to your relationship. You can always pick up where you left off tomorrow.

Cats need training too. Much of what I've written in this chapter will work for felines as well. Many people refuse to train their cats to walk on a leash, to stay off the furniture, or to stay off the counters. They feel it's not natural for cats to obey. I disagree. With proper motivation, consistency in training, and corrections as necessary, cats can also be well-trained — if you are willing to put in the necessary time and effort.

I correct my cats with a loud noise, or with a squirt from a water bottle. If you have more than one cat, make sure that the noise or water only affects the misbehaving kitty — if the other cat is doing something correct, such as using the litter box, and gets startled, he may associate the correction with that act.

Rewards for your cat can be anything from a scratch behind the ear, to a treat, to a play session with a toy. The key is to find out what motivates her, and use it to get the behavior that you want.

Equipment for training:

- six-foot leather leash (for advanced work and work such as heeling)

- twelve-foot web leash (for recalls on lead, and preliminary heeling work)

- training collar

- motivational items, such as food, toys, or balls

Questions to ask before training:

Given his choice, what would my dog prefer to do above anything else? The answer to this should help you determine what motivates him.

Does my dog display extreme discomfort or pain when my veterinarian gives him a shot, or does he barely flinch?

Does he yelp if his tail or toe is accidentally stepped on?

If I squeeze the webbing between his toes, does a slight pressure make him wince? These answers should help you determine your dog's pain tolerance, which can be useful for assessing the types of corrections that will be most beneficial.

What are my goals for training my pet?

What am I willing to do to achieve them?

Use the space below to record notes about your training sessions.
Include the date, what you worked on, and how the session went.
Keeping a log can help you pinpoint problems before they develop. A log can also serve as a motivational tool for you — when
you are discouraged or frustrated, review it to see how much
progress you have made. Finally, a log makes it more difficult for
you to "cheat" when training — it shows in black and white
whether you've been putting the necessary time in to succeed.

_____

_____

_____

_____

_____

_____

_____

_____

_____

Training

Training

Training

Top 10 Tips

1. **Know your pet — and yourself.** Not every pet has the potential for high performance, and not every owner has the time and energy to put into performance training. If all you want is a reasonably well-trained pet, recognize that and accept it as a valid choice.

2. **Most pets aren't prodigies.** Just as you wouldn't expect a toddler to master algebra, you shouldn't expect perfection in puppies and kittens. They need time to mature before they can handle formal training.

3. **Find a good instructor.** Working with someone who's trained animals before can help you avoid problems and speed up your pet's learning cycle.

4. **Training time is bonding time.** Don't look on it as a chore — view it as a way to spend quality time with your pet, and strengthen your relationship.

5. **Master motivation.** It's one of the quickest, easiest tricks for good training.

6. **Learn your pet's lusts.** Food, toys, playtime, praise — find out what your pet loves, and use it to reward him during training.

7. **Corrections aren't cruel — if they are done correctly.** Correct only if you are sure your pet knows what you want and isn't doing it. The correction should be appropriate, swift, and concise — no nagging allowed.

8. **Be fair.** Don't train when you are in a bad mood, and be consistent when enforcing the rules.

9. **Don't make excuses.** If your pet knows what a command means, he should follow through no matter what distractions tempt him. If he only listens when nothing else is happening, what's the point?

10. **Practice, practice, practice.** You'll wind up with a perfect pet and a bond nothing can break.

5

Working With Your Veterinarian

Dog may be man's best friend, but who is the best friend of the dog? Hopefully, it's you — but running a close second should be your veterinarian.

When I moved cross-country a few years ago, the first thing I did after finding a physician for my family was to find a veterinarian for my pets. I met with several before making my decision, and I've never regretted it.

The veterinarian I use now is knowledgeable, calm, and experienced. He or someone at the clinic will take my calls at any hour. Although he practices traditional veterinarian medicine, he's comfortable discussing alternative methods, and is

"The key to a good relationship between vet and owner is communication," says Michael Good, DVM.

willing to refer me to a holistic practitioner if I request one. Best of all, my pets seem to genuinely enjoy visiting him.

Finding this type of relationship with a veterinarian requires a little work on the part of pet owners, but it's worth it. "The key to a good relationship between vet and owner is communication," said Michael Good, DVM. "The vet needs to ask what the owner's concerns are, and take the time to listen to those concerns." At the same time, the owner needs to be able to articulate what is happening with his or her pet.

Like any relationship, the one between vet and pet owner takes time to develop — and the one between pet and vet can take even longer. But there are things you can do to help strengthen that alliance:

Shop around. Ask friends, breeders, and trainers who they use for their pets. What do they like about their veterinarian? Does he or she take the time to listen to them? Does their pet seem relaxed around them? Is their vet willing to refer them, if necessary? Does the clinic have emergency hours? How close is the clinic to your home? Could you get there quickly if your pet had a problem? The answers to these questions can help you find the veterinarian who best meets your needs.

You may find that you prefer to use one vet for simple vaccinations, and another for emergencies. If that's the case, make sure the emergency vet has an updated file on your pet, including a history of all shots, medications, and allergies.

Take time to talk. Once you've decided on a vet, set up an appointment with him or her. Use this visit as a time to introduce your pet and the vet. Now is the time to ask the vet about his or her experiences with your breed, to chat about diet, and to discuss any ongoing concerns you may have about your pet's health.

Bring any paperwork you may already have, such as records of vaccinations, so that the vet can create an up-to-date file on your pet. Let the vet weigh your pet, and check his or her teeth and nails. Keep this first visit simple and upbeat. It's a nice way for your pet to form some positive associations with the vet, which will make future visits go more smoothly.

Do drop in. Once you've had your preliminary meeting, bring your pet by the clinic occasionally just to visit. "I don't know any vet that doesn't welcome a client coming through the door just to say hi," said Dr. Good. Let the staff give your dog a treat, or put him on the scale to check his weight. The goal is to establish the clinic as a good place to go.

My two German Shepherd Dogs love their visits to the vet. When other dogs are cowering under the seats in the waiting room, my dogs are pulling at the leash to get into the examining room. They want to see their buddy the vet and get at the treats they know are waiting for them. This kind of attitude didn't happen overnight — it took several nonthreatening visits. But the time I put in initially makes trips to the vet much easier today.

Explore alternative therapies. I'm a big believer in holistic medicine. I've used acupuncture on my adult dog, Jano, with terrific results, and researched various herbs extensively before adding them to Mrs. Allen's SHED-STOP. But I would never have pursued either acupuncture or herbal medicine without the support of my vet. In fact, Mrs. Allen's SHED-STOP has been endorsed by veterinarians, many of

Grooming sessions can help keep your pet in top-notch condition between visits to the vet.

whom actually recommend it to their clients whose pets are experiencing shedding or skin problems.

Before trying any alternative method of treatment, discuss it with your veterinarian. He or she can point out its benefits and drawbacks, and let you know how it will work in conjunction with treatments you may already be using.

If your vet doesn't practice the type of treatment you are interested in exploring, ask for a referral. "Vets specialize in lots of things," said Dr. Good, who practices in Atlanta, Georgia. "We have a list of practitioners and other resources in town, and we'll refer our clients to them if they are interested." Massage therapists, chiropractors, behavioral specialists, herbalists — all can benefit your pet, provided you are using qualified individuals. Your vet can help you to find them.

Schedule regular visits. Lots of pet owners only go to the doctor when they have a problem, and they only bring their pets to the vet when they need shots or they have an emergency. But as with people, routine checkups can provide big benefits.

"We had a dog come in today that had a heart murmur," said Dr. Good. The owner hadn't noticed any unusual symptoms — in fact, the dog had only come in for a bath. But the vet on duty said a friendly hello by way of a quick checkup, and caught the signs. "If, by proper management of the problem, we can help that pet live to the age of 15 instead of 12, we've just added twenty-five percent more years to his life," said Good.

Many vets now offer a package deal, where routine shots are combined with regular checkups. It's a bargain that I believe is well worth taking advantage of. Health insurance for pets is another innovation that can make visits and treatment more affordable. If you are interested, talk with your vet about coverage requirements.

Perform preventive care. Regularly examine your pet for moles, lumps, or other abnormalities. Check ears and eyes for unusual discharges. Monitor your pet's eating, sleeping, and elimination patterns. If there are changes, bring them to your vet's attention immediately. Many pet diseases have early warning signs, but you have to be paying attention to see them.

Bring bratty behavior to your vet's attention. If your cat suddenly starts mistaking your hardwood floors for the litter box, or if your dog seems unusually grumpy, don't just assume that you are being tested. There could be a medical reason for your pet's "bad" behavior.

For example, lower urinary track disease can make it difficult for cats to use the litter box. And an inner ear infection can make even the kindest canine cranky. So if you notice any deviant behavior, schedule an examination. Explain to your vet what you've noticed, and work with him or her to determine whether there is a medical reason for the changes.

Remember that dealing with pets is often like dealing with small children, in that they can't tell you what's wrong. It may take several visits to the vet, and careful observation on your part, before there's a diagnosis. If, after several efforts, a medical problem is ruled out, ask your vet for help in changing the behavioral problem. Behavior modification may be effective. If

Different pets may have different bathing requirements. Our shampoo and cologne can keep any pet fresh-smelling.

not, veterinary medicine has progressed to the point that the Food and Drug Administration recently approved the first two drugs designed specifically for treating pets with behavioral problems associated with aging. If your vet can't help, ask to be referred to someone who specializes in animal behavior.

Give senior citizens special attention. Experts agree that pets are living longer, better lives because of advances in nutrition and medicine. But owners may fail to realize that, even though Fido is still frisky, he's a senior citizen.

Your vet can help your older pet live a longer, healthier life — but only if you make sure to schedule regular checkups. Older pets should be examined at least once every six months. Typical health problems that plague older pets include arthritis, hearing and vision loss, heart disease, and arthritis.

Your vet can help you manage these problems by providing special care, such as nutritional counseling, medications, or, in extreme cases, surgery. But monitoring can help catch problems early, eliminating the need for more serious treatment.

It's particularly important to keep your senior pet's vaccinations current. His or her immune system may not be as strong as it once was, making him or her more susceptible to disease. You may also want to talk with your vet about having baseline blood and urine tests done. Later tests can then be measured against them, helping your vet spot diseases in their earliest stage.

It's also important to watch older pets for behavioral changes, such as aimless wandering, loss of house-training, and lack of familiarity with well-known surroundings or people. These can indicate a deterioration of cognitive abilities. Your vet may be able to help you slow or control these symptoms, expanding your pet's enjoyment of life.

Finally, work with your vet to establish good dental hygiene for your pet. Kidney and heart failure are two common problems in older pets, and keeping teeth clean can have a major impact on your dog's health in these areas. Ask your vet to clean your pet's teeth on a regular basis. (For some pets, this may require anesthesia). At home, follow the schedule of dental care that your vet recommends.

Work with, not against your vet. It's difficult for vets to work on animals that are frightened, disobedient, or plain old squirmy. "Obviously, an obedient, compliant pet that allows us to interact with it is easier to examine," said Dr. Good.

You can help your vet by teaching your dog basic obedience skills, such as standing on command. Get your cat used to being gently handled. And have both pets become comfortable with having their teeth, paws, and ears examined.

You can also help your vet by following any medical instructions he or she gives. "It's frustrating when owners won't do the things we ask them to do to keep their pets healthy," he said. Simple things, such as giving heartworm pills for the prescribed amount of time, or changing bandages as asked, can have a big impact on your pet's health.

Last but not least, don't be suckered into pleas for help from your pet in the examining room. One cat I know always acts as if she's on death row when she's on the examining table. She howls, moans, and meows pathetically, and when that fails, she hisses. Her owner has finally wised up to the fact that her pet has great acting skills, and has stopped pleading with the vet to stop torturing her.

That doesn't mean you need to put up with someone who is overly rough with your pet — speak up if you feel your pet is being mistreated, and look for another vet if you are unhappy with the way your animal is handled. But pets can be big babies when they are unhappy, and owners can make the examination more difficult by rushing to "rescue" them when in fact there's nothing wrong.

Use your vet as a resource. Vets aren't just there for medical problems. They can help you find a pet that will meet your needs and expectations. They can refer you to obedience trainers, behavioral specialists, and clubs and activities that revolve around pet ownership. Most importantly, they can help improve and extend your pet's life. But they can only help you if you establish a relationship that's built on trust and communication.

Equipment for a trip to the veterinarian:

- collar (depending on your pet's temperament, you may choose to use a buckle or training collar)

- harness or leash

- cat carrier

- treats

Use this section as a log to record your pet's health history and to jot down questions to ask your vet during your next visit.

Vaccinations

What given   Date given

_____

_____

_____

_____

_____

Allergic reactions

_____

_____

Substance Reaction

_____

_____

Unusual behavior to ask the vet about:

Other questions to ask:

Instructions for giving medication or other treatment:

Top 10 Tips

1. **Shop around.** Ask friends and breeders which veterinarians they use, and why they recommend him or her.

2. **Take time to talk.** Before you sign on with one veterinarian, schedule an introductory appointment to make sure you agree on methods of care.

3. **Do drop in.** Bring your pet to the clinic occasionally just to visit, get weighed, and receive a treat. The goal is to build positive associations with the vet.

4. **Explore alternative therapies.** Acupuncture, massage, and herbal treatments may all benefit your pet. Before seeking a practitioner, ask your vet for recommendations.

5. **Schedule regular visits.** They may help your vet head off health problems before they start.

6. **Perform preventive care.** In-between trips to the vet, monitor your pet for unusual symptoms, such as odd discharges or loss of appetite. If the symptoms persist, contact your vet.

7. **Bring bratty behavior to your vet's attention.** If Fido suddenly starts snapping, or Fluffy misses the litter box, there could be a medical reason behind the changes.

8. **Give senior citizens special attention.** Careful monitoring and care, such as frequent check-ups and attention to diet and exercise, can help prevent problems associated with aging.

9. **Work with, not against your vet.** Follow his or her instructions when it comes to taking medication, restricting treats, and providing exercise.

10. **Use your vet as a resource.** Vets can be a pet's second-best friend. They can provide information on diet and nutrition, recommend obedience trainers, behavioral specialists, and pet clubs and activities, and even help you find a pet that will fit in with your family. All you have to do is ask.

6

Nutrition, Nutrition, Nutrition

"**I won't feed my animals anything I wouldn't eat myself.**" I've made this statement on radio shows, on television, and during interviews, and it's one that I truly believe. People who aren't pet lovers may think I'm crazy, but I've personally tested every single product I've ever given my animals.

I'm a strong believer in the power of good nutrition for both the human and animal members of my family. I've seen what a good diet can do for my pets' coats, teeth, and energy level, and I would never feed them anything but the best possible food. Sometimes, that means feeding them what I'm eating, as in the case of Mrs. Allen's SHED-STOP.

Mrs. Allen's SHED-STOP® has the ASPCA® (American Society for the Prevention Of Cruelty to Animals) Seal of Approval — it contains the optimal ratio of omega 6/omega 3 healthy fatty acids.

You can take pride in knowing that a portion of all our proceeds goes to the ASPCA!

My secret formula was derived centuries ago by shepherds in the Austro-Hungarian Empire. It was handed down to my grandfather, who not only fed it to his dogs and cats, but drank it himself. He passed this tradition on to me, just as I will do with my own children.

Just as when my grandfather made it for me, I make SHED-STOP for pets from only the highest-quality ingredients. The oils used are premium grade — better than some found in gourmet salad dressings. All of the ingredients are natural, without harmful preservatives or chemicals.

Made with sunflower, safflower, olive, and soya oils, along with Vitamins B-complex, A and E, and Zinc, SHED-STOP is unique because it works from the inside out, giving pets the nutrients they need to grow healthy, glowing coats.

Well-balanced pet foods have some of these nutrients. But by adding them as a dietary supplement, you boost your pet's intake, ensuring that there's an adequate supply of nutrients for healthy hair and skin. And healthy hair and skin means less shedding, which translates to less time spent cleaning and more time for fun with your pet!

Of course, SHED-STOP isn't a cure-all, although hundreds of pet owners have written to me about the fabulous improvements they've seen in the quality of their pet's coats, skin, and even arthritis after using it. And there's only so much SHED-STOP can do if your pet's diet is poor to begin with.

I'm not an expert, and the following steps I've discovered for improving my pets' health through nutrition, while "food for thought," are no substitute for consulting with your veterinarian.

Do your homework. There are several different schools of thought on what is the best diet for pets. Before you make a decision, make sure you are making an educated one. Read one of the excellent books on the market about pet nutrition, talk with experts, or use the internet to do some research. Switching foods or diets without a plan can cause problems.

For example, one approach advocates feeding pets raw foods, including meats, bones, and vegetables. Proponents swear that this type of diet produces animals in glowing good health, with vibrant coats and plenty of energy. But there must be a balance in the types of food you feed, or problems may result. For example, too much meat can give your pet loose stools. Too little protein can make your pet lethargic. Some grains can cause rashes called "hot spots."

Even commercial pet foods can cause problems. Make sure you read the label of every can or bag you buy. What are you feeding? Ingredients must be listed in order of quantity, so the first few ingredients are the primary sources of nutrition for your pet. Since cats and dogs are primarily carnivores, make sure that meat is high up on the label. Avoid foods that contain lots of fillers, such as rice or wheat.

Also make it a point to ask others what they feed their pets. If you see a dog or cat in glowing good health, with bright eyes, a shiny coat, and loads of energy, find out what it's eating.

Proper nutrition is crucial for your pet's good health.

Most breeders and owners are happy to share this type of information.

Talk with your vet. It's a good idea to run any dietary changes past your veterinarian. He or she can help you make an educated choice about what's best for your pet. In addition, if you are interested in pursuing an alternative choice, such as a raw food diet, your vet should be able to put you in touch with a qualified expert, who can help you devise a diet that will meet your pet's needs.

Make changes gradually. Some pets can switch from one food to another, or one diet to another, without any problems. Others may experience discomfort or side effects, such as gas or loose stools. To be safe, make changes gradually, over the course of a few days or even a week. Start by mixing a small portion of the new food into the old; gradually increase the amount until your pet has made a complete switch.

Remember that your pet is an individual. Dogs and cats, puppies and kittens, all have different nutritional needs. Other differences depend upon the age, condition, and activity level of your pet. Young, active puppies, for example, may need to be fed more frequently than mature, staid adults.

These variances are why we make different types of SHED-STOP; one for dogs and puppies, another for cats and kittens, and still another for ferrets and horses. Cats, for example, can't synthesize the essential fatty acid arachadonic acid from linoleic and linoleic acids. For that reason, our cat and kitten formula provides arachadonic acid through fish oils. Dogs receive this acid, which is one key to good coats, through other oils.

There are other factors besides breed to consider when contemplating your pet's nutritional needs. If your pet has an extremely active temperament and is never still, he may need more food than a pet of the same breed who spends most of his time on the sofa. If you take your pet hiking or running with you, he's also going to need more fuel to keep up.

Even the same pet can have different nutritional needs from month to month. Gabe, a police dog I know, usually gets several cups of dry dog food a day. But in the summertime, when he's at his most active, his handler adds a can of moist food to each meal. Otherwise, Gabe's weight drops off.

You are the best judge of the type and amount of food that your pet requires. Be observant:

Look him over carefully. Are his eyes bright and alert? Is his coat shiny and full? Does he have plenty of energy, or does he mope around the house?

Feel from her head to her tail. Run your hands over your pet's body. Does her coat feel soft or coarse? Is she well-muscled and firm? Or does she have rolls of fat around her waist?

The answers to these questions can provide clues to the type and amount of food your pet needs.

Seniors need special care. Older pets may be more likely to suffer from diseases such as renal failure, which is irreversible and fatal. Special diets can help your pet live a longer and healthier life. For example, Omega-3 fatty acids can help decrease blood pressure on the kidneys, which can slow the progression of renal

High quality snacks can compliment your pet's diet — just don't overdo it!

damage. As your pet ages, talk with your veterinarian about the diet that's best for his needs. And feel good about feeding seniors SHED-STOP, since it contains Omega-3 and 6 fatty acids in optimal proportions.

Avoid unnecessary or frequent food changes. Once you've found a diet that works for your dog, stick with it. Constantly alternating foods can give your pet an upset stomach, or can create a finicky eater.

Stay away from too many treats. If your dog is eating a well-balanced diet, too many snacks can throw it out of whack. Plus, many of the treats we like to feed our pets, such as candy, cookies, and the like aren't good for them (or us)!

On the other hand, I know one breeder who takes her dog to a fast food establishment every time he wins a show. The dog gets a burger, the owner gets french fries, and everyone has a good day. I wouldn't advise making this a regular event, though!

Supplement with Vitamin C. Although dogs and cats do naturally create Vitamin C within their bodies, supplementing can help strengthen their immune systems. I give my dogs a natural source of vitamin C, which is contained in SHED-STOP. If you are interested in feeding Vitamin C by itself, start with very low doses and gradually increase the amount. Talk with your vet about what level of Vitamin C can best benefit your pet.

Garlic is great! The nutritional and protective qualities of garlic are just starting to be discovered, although garlic has been used medicinally by humans for centuries. Some studies have shown that components of the herb may have cancer-fighting properties. Others have found that garlic may have the ability to reduce the risk of blood clots — or lower cholesterol levels.

What does this mean for your pet? Although most garlic studies have been conducted on humans, many pet owners swear by the benefits of "the stinking rose," even claiming it can repel fleas. But be cautious before introducing the smelly stuff to your pet, particularly cats; there's some evidence that a form of anemia has been linked to garlic consumption in felines. Talk with your vet or a qualified herbalist, and don't give more than one-half to one clove per day. If your pet won't consume garlic in its raw form, sprinkle liquid garlic or garlic granules on top of his food and mix well.

Add antioxidants for a boost. Vitamin E and other antioxidants, such as Vitamin B complex and beta carotene, can help boost the immune system of pets, particularly older ones. A strong immune system makes it easier to fight off infections. I take Vitamin E myself, and I add it to my dogs' diet, along with B-complex and Vitamin A, in the form of SHED-STOP.

Don't accept shedding. It's true that shedding is a normal process that occurs seasonally in both cats and dogs. But constant, "nuisance" shedding that goes on year-round isn't necessary. For many pet owners, it is one of the biggest drawbacks to fully enjoying a relationship with their animals.

One of the major controllable factors contributing to shedding is nutrition, which impacts both hair growth and loss. SHED-STOP contains the vitamins, minerals,

This golden retriever's bright eyes and shiny coat are the result of good nutrition.

oils, and other ingredients that can help you eliminate or reduce nonseasonal shedding. It's also recommended and used by veterinarians.

"I have found SHED-STOP to work very well for many of my clients," said Dr. Lila C. Windus, DVM. "What seems to set it apart from other products is Lecithin, an emulsifier necessary for every tissue in the body. Due to this fact it might also aid in the inflammation of joints, nerves, etc., as well as skin inflammation."

SHED-STOP is also set apart from other products in that it is completely natural, safe, and pleasant-tasting to pets — you don't have to fight to get them to eat it. Combined with proper nutrition, SHED-STOP can make pet ownership more fun and less work. And isn't that what owning a pet is all about?

Try It Yourself

Questions to ask:

How does my pet's coat and general health appear? Is his coat shiny? Are his eyes bright? Or are coat and eyes dull? Does he shed year-round, no matter what the season? Is he lively and active, or does he seem tired all the time? Record your impressions in the space below.

Now run your hands over your pet's body. How does he feel? Can you feel muscle, or is it buried under a roll of fat? Does his coat feel healthy, or brittle? Record your impressions in the space below.

For the next week, record what you feed your pet. Make sure you include everything, including table scraps. Write down the quantity of food as well. At the end of the week, review the information. Is your pet getting more treats than you originally thought? Does everyone in the family feed the same amount of food at each meal? Are you giving in to his reproachful paw at the dinner table?

Finally, take a moment to read the label on your pet's bag or can of food. What are the primary ingredients? Are they fillers, or actual sources of nutrition, such as meat or fish?

Armed with the information above, talk with your veterinarian about the optimal diet for your pet. Before significantly reducing or increasing the amount you feed, get your vet's okay. Do the same before radically changing your pet's diet. After making changes, record your pet's condition over one-month intervals. Has he lost weight? Is his coat glossier? Can you feel a difference when you run your hands over his ribs? Because you see your dog or cat every day, it can be difficult to notice changes. That's where recording and comparing the results can give you tangible proof that the diet you've chosen is working.

Top 10 Tips

1. **Do your homework.** Before making changes in your pet's diet, research the different schools of thought on pet food. Switching diets without a plan can lead to problems.

2. **Talk with your vet.** Ask him or her for input on any changes you are planning to make.

3. **Make changes gradually.** Sudden switches in food can cause side effects such as intestinal discomfort, gas, or loose stools.

4. **Remember that your pet is an individual.** His breed, activity level, and age all impact his nutritional needs.

5. **Be observant.** Check your pet's condition regularly. If his coat is dull, or if you feel ribs or rolls of fat around his middle, you may want to consider changing the amount and/or type of food you feed.

6. **Seniors need special care.** A good diet can help prevent or reduce problems common to older pets, such as kidney failure.

7. **Avoid unnecessary food changes.** Once you find something that works, stick with it.

8. **Stay away from too many treats.** They can make your pet obese and cause health problems. If you do feed your pet special snacks, be sure to factor them into his overall caloric allotment for the day.

9. **Consider supplementing your pet's diet with vitamins such as Vitamin C and Vitamin E.** Found in Mrs. Allen's SHED-STOP, these vitamins have long been touted as immune system boosters. If you plan to give your pet vitamins outside of SHED-STOP, discuss the best dose with your vet.

10. **Don't accept shedding.** It's true that shedding is a normal process that occurs seasonally in both cats and dogs. But constant, "nuisance" shedding that goes on year-round isn't necessary. SHED-STOP contains the vitamins, minerals, oils, and other ingredients that can help you eliminate or reduce nonseasonal shedding.

7

Stepping Out

People weren't built to sit on sofas all day, and neither were their pets. In the wild, dogs and cats would be hunting, foraging for food, fighting, defending their territory ... all active pursuits. Domestic life has brought some advantages, but it also has at least one big drawback: there's not much of a challenge in chasing down a bag of kibble.

Many pets spend most of their days and nights sleeping. They get lots of treats and food, and as a result often wind up looking like fur-covered footstools with legs. But obesity isn't the only problem inactive pets face. They may be restless, whiny, and bored, which can lead to destructive behavior.

My personal theory is that a tired pet is a good pet. Involve your dog or cat in an activity that will stimulate both mind and body, and he's much less likely to get into trouble, simply because he won't have the energy. One local rescue group for a particularly intense breed of dog tells potential "parents" that regular exercise is a condition of adoption. They find that the dogs have far less behavioral problems when they are put through their paces. The workouts engage both their minds and their bodies, and the result is a happier, healthier pet.

But exercise isn't just a way to curb negative tendencies in your pet — it's also a way to strengthen your relationship and have fun. A simple walk can be an enormous treat for a housebound cat or dog, and they will associate the positive experience with you.

We regularly take our two German Shepherd Dogs for long hikes in a nearby state forest. The moment we pull into the parking lot, their tails are up and they can't wait to get out. A good two-hour romp guarantees both a quiet ride home and time to sleep in the next morning — the dogs are usually too tired to wake us up!

There are all kinds of activities you can do with your pet that will provide exercise, fun, and entertainment for the two of you. Be creative. Check with your local newspaper, dog or cat club, or research web sites to get ideas. The following tips can help you get started:

Check with your vet before beginning a regular exercise routine. This is particularly important for older pets. A two-mile hike the first time out might be fine for your young dog,

Trainer Richard Crane competes in Schutzhund to keep his dogs in shape and reduce behavioral problems.

but could really be difficult for a senior citizen. Puppies should get your vet's okay, too. Running and jumping can stress fragile bones and joints that haven't finished growing yet.

Your vet will be able to give you guidelines for how much to exercise and how often. Depending on the area of the country you live in, you might also want to ask about safety precautions, such as a Lyme Disease vaccine, that can help your pet avoid illness.

Protect your pet. If you are hiking, get a reflective vest for your pet. They are relatively inexpensive, and make him more visible to hunters and cars in the area. These vests may also be a wise investment if you walk at dusk or at night.

In addition to reflective vests, I attach small bells to my dogs' collars when out hiking. These bells warn other people and animals in the area of our approach. They also help me keep track of our dogs should they slip from my sight for a moment.

Finally, make sure your pet's collar has tags with your phone number and address in case you are separated. I use leather collars on both of my dogs. Should they get lost and become caught on something, the leather wouldn't become a noose — it would give to the pressure. NEVER leave a "choke" or training collar on an unsupervised pet, particularly when hiking or performing other activities. The rings could get caught on a branch, in a crack on your deck, or even on another dog, and could choke your pet.

Start slowly. You may be an accomplished runner, but if Fido is just starting out, don't expect him to go the distance with you. If your pet isn't used to regular exercise, break him in gradually, in short, 15 to 20 minute segments. Avoid exercising during the hottest part of the day, and provide plenty of fresh water before and after.

Train, train, train. A pet who walks well on a leash and responds to basic commands will enjoy exercise more than one who is continually choking himself by pulling too hard, or constantly being reprimanded. Cats should learn to walk on a lead before you venture outdoors, not after. At the bare minimum, dogs should learn not to pull. Ideally, they should also know how to heel. These basic steps can make exercise a lot more enjoyable for you and for them.

Find an activity your pet enjoys. A friend of mine has three Australian Shepherds. Annie, the female, loves agility. Gridley prefers herding. Powder is my friend's obedience dog. Although the dogs share a similar genetic makeup, they all have preferences that became evident the first few times they were exposed to the particular activity.

It may sound crazy at first — finding an activity just for your pet. But look at it this way: Most of these sports provide good exercise for people as well as pets. In addition, animal activities can be a nice way to meet other people, and can be a fun, healthy way to spend a Saturday afternoon, particularly for families with children or teenagers.

If you are unsure of where to start, research your pet's breed. Dogs from breeds that were used for herding may be eligible to compete in herding trials, done with sheep or ducks. Hounds that hunt by sight may be eligible for lure-coursing, in which they chase a plastic bag or 'lure,' around an outdoor course. All breeds are eligible for agility, a sport that involves a timed run around an obstacle course that includes A-frames, hoops, and catwalks.

If your pet isn't a pure-bred, don't despair. Some clubs will let dogs of any ancestry join and compete in events. Others, like the American Kennel Club, require dogs without papers to have an Indefinite Listing Privilege (I.L.P.). This is fairly simple to obtain — it simply means that your dog has been identified as looking like a particular breed. Contact the A.K.C. for an application, and return it with a filing fee and photos of the dog. Once you have your pet's I.L.P. number, you can compete in performance events such as obedience.

Finding activities for cats can be more difficult — there are few, if any, organized events for them. You may need to get creative with toys and activities. A crinkly paper bag, a string drawn through the tall grass in your yard, a feather duster attached to a fishing rod that's kept just out of range, can all provide exercise and entertainment.

Not all exercise activities have to be organized, either. Simply playing frisbee or fetch with your pet can be enough. Another favorite game at our house is hide and seek. My children will hide, either indoors or on our property. We make sure the dogs see them go, but don't let them follow. After counting to 20, the dogs are released, and race around trying to unearth our giggling girls. There are a couple of keys to making this work: our dogs know not to mouth our daughters, no matter how intense the fun gets. And our daughters have a good

Play sessions with other pets are a fun way to provide exercise.

grounding on what's acceptable behavior around dogs. We've taught them not to run from the dogs, for example — although our two pets are fine with them, other dogs might respond by seeing them as prey, and knock them down or mouth them.

Try toys. There are all kinds of toys on the market for pets, and at least a few of them offer a good workout for brain and body. One of my favorites is a cube or ball in which food is placed. The pet can bat it around with its nose and paws, and the food is gradually released. These toys are made for both dogs and cats — just make sure to subtract the food that you use in the toy from their daily ration.

Scratching posts, although not really "toys," can also provide hours of activity for kitties. Watch to see what, where, and how your cat likes to scratch. Does she reach high, or make long, horizontal scratches around the house? What type of surface does she prefer? To keep scratching from being destructive, purchase a scratching post that matches what you've observed, and put it in an area that your cat is likely to spend time in — the kitchen, a sunny spot in the window, a corner of the bedroom where she hangs out. Don't relegate the scratching post to the basement — it's unlikely it will get much use there.

Scratching posts don't have to be fancy, either. An old piece of carpet that's reversed and fastened to a strong, stable post can be enough. The key is whether it's something your cat will enjoy, and only observation of her particular habits can tell you that.

Focus on fun. Whether you are taking a walk or competing in an agility match, it should be an enjoyable experience — for both you and your pet. Constant corrections, commands, or just dirty looks from you take a lot of the fun out of the event.

It's particularly important to focus on the positive if your pet is trying a new experience. The first time you take your cat for a walk outside, for example, isn't the time to be jerking the lead or yelling at her for rolling and trying to remove the harness.

A more effective approach is to praise your pet when he does something well, such as hop over a jump or walk well on-lead for a few feet. Build your pet's confidence and he'll want to try it again the next time.

Don't get hung up on who's doing better than you when you're competing, either. Agility, herding, competitive frisbee, or whatever sport you choose to explore all have one thing in common — at their core, they are meant to provide a fun way for pets and their owners to interact. If you do well, great. If you don't, it's just an excuse for you to spend more time training, having fun, and getting it right.

Be considerate. There are certain social responsibilities that come with owning a pet. When exercising your animal, be prepared to clean up after him. Irresponsible pet owners are one reason many people hate to see dogs in public areas such as parks. Your actions don't just determine how you are judged — they also influence how people view pet owners in general. So do the responsible thing and bring plastic bags along.

Consideration doesn't just extend to clean-up duty, either. When out in public with your pet, obey local leash laws. If pets are allowed off-leash, make sure your pet will respond to voice commands. If he won't, work with him until he does, but don't let him off leash until then. And if your dog is aggressive toward other animals, it may be smarter to keep him leashed at all times.

Dog parks can be a great way to exercise your pet and get some socialization for both of you. But don't get so wrapped up in the conversation with other owners that you neglect to keep an eye on your own dog. If your pet is off-leash, it's your responsibility to supervise his actions. Anything else is just asking for trouble.

This is also true during events and practice runs for activities such as agility. Nothing is more annoying than having six dogs all swarming over the same obstacles at the same time. It's also dangerous — an animal could get injured on the equipment, or a fight could erupt. Most clubs have an informal rule of thumb — only one animal off-lead at a time. It's a smart standard, and one worth observing.

Try It Yourself

Equipment for exercise:

- buckle collar

- identification tags

- long web leash

- reflective vest

- water for long hikes or play sessions

Questions to ask:

What type of activities does my pet seem to enjoy?
For example, if you have a Shetland Sheepdog that tries to herd people, you might consider herding lessons. A cat that constantly stalks shadows might benefit from a motorized toy.

Is this activity safe?
The biggest rule of thumb I consider when trying a new activity is whether it's safe for the animals and people involved. Is the activity healthy, or will it damage my pet's joints and bones? Can it be done in an area free of traffic? Will the pet learn behaviors that might be dangerous later, such as mouthing or scratching people? These are all factors to consider before exposing your pet to a new activity.

What are my goals for this activity?
Do I want to meet new people, tire out my pet, or get him in shape? Do I want to simply pursue this activity on a recreational level, or do I want to compete? The answers to these questions can help you decide whether to find a club or group that shares your interests, or simply pursue the activity on your own.

Use the space below to record notes about your pet's exercise sessions. Include the date, the duration, what activity was done, and comments about your pet's reaction to the session. These notes can help you to pinpoint whether your pet enjoys the activity, identify any injuries that occur, and serve as a record of his improvement in a particular sport. Finally, months or years from now, your notes will be a reminder of the times that you and your pet enjoyed together.

Exercise

Top 10 Tips

1. **A tired pet is a good pet.** A pet that's raring to go and doesn't have an appropriate channel for that energy is bound to get in trouble. Exercise provides a safe, constructive outlet.

2. **Check with your vet before beginning a regular exercise routine.** This is particularly important for young animals, whose bones may not be fully formed, and for senior citizens who are out of shape.

3. **Protect your pet.** Make sure he's up-to-date on all his shots, has been treated to fend off pests such as ticks, and is wearing a sturdy collar with tags or other identification. A reflective vest may also help if you are hiking.

4. **Start slowly.** Build up to longer periods of exercise over time.

5. **Train, train, train.** Keeping control is essential for safe exercise.

6. **Find an activity your pet enjoys.** He'll be more likely to want to participate with you.

7. **Try toys.** Exercise doesn't have to be an organized event, such as agility. Pets can get a good workout by simply chasing a ball or toy mouse.

8. **Focus on fun.** Winning ribbons in a sport such as lure coursing can be enjoyable, but should take second place to simply having a good time with your pet.

9. **Be considerate.** If you can't control your pet, keep him on-lead until you can. And make sure you clean up after him.

10. **Bring plenty of water.** Pets can get dehydrated just like people. Water and shade can make exercise safer and more enjoyable.

8

De-Stressing Your Pet

Imagine waking up one day in a place where no one understood you — literally. The people you meet speak a different language. They eat foods that are different from what you eat, have different interests, and practice hygienic habits that you just can't fathom.

Despite these differences, you decide to try and make friends with these strangers. After all, you figure, you may be here for some time. So you wait and watch. One day, you see the woman whose house you are in get ready to eat. She mixes a bunch of foods together that smell great, although you aren't sure what they are. When you try to get closer, she pushes you away.

In an effort to be friendly, you offer her part of a chocolate bar. When the woman sees what you are eating, she looks horrified, snatches it away from you — and shoves you out the door.

Later, when she lets you back into the house, you're thrilled and excited, quite willing to forgive the mix-up about the chocolate bar. You've spent the last few hours trying to clean up under a hose outside, so you are feeling reasonably presentable and ready to try again. But when the woman gets close to you, she sniffs and wrinkles her nose. The next thing you know, you are back outside again, only this time she's with you — and she's scrubbing you from head to toe with some strong-smelling stuff you can't stand.

When you finally get away from her, you run through the house in search of a towel. The only one you can find is hanging on the wall, so you grab it and start to dry off. The woman

Socialize puppies and kittens early on to get them used to all kinds of situations.

sees you and starts screaming. She grabs the towel away from you, then starts thwacking you with it.

Forget being friends, you think as you run for cover. This person's crazy!

If this actually happened to you, it's likely that you'd be bewildered — and highly stressed from trying to understand and communicate with someone who seems to view your every natural action with suspicion or distaste.

Your pets live in a world that's similar to the one you encountered in our imaginary scenario. Contrary to popular belief, dogs and cats aren't little people in fuzzy suits. They are animals, with animal natures, who often live in an unnatural world of our making.

They don't "speak" our language, although they may come to understand some of it. What they consider edible doesn't always meet our standards. Despite our preference for cleanliness, most pets would be happy if "bath" were considered a four-letter word. And they often don't comprehend the way we act.

And just like people, pets can get stressed in situations where they don't understand what's expected of them. In our imaginary scenario, it wouldn't take more than a few days of this kind of treatment for you to be surreptitiously sneaking aspirin for stress headaches, or pulling out your hair. You might lose your appetite, or develop nervous tics.

Pets react to stress much the same way. They may start licking themselves more often, start gnawing on their paws, or lose their appetite. They may claw the furniture or the curtains, hide beneath the bed, or start shedding excessively.

Your pet can't tell you why it's stressed — as a pet owner, it's your responsibility to figure it out, and help your pet deal with stressful situations. Keep in mind, too, that some pets deal better with stressful triggers than others. A dog that's been raised in a healthy environment, that's been exposed to lots of people and places, and that comes from calm, well-socialized parents, will probably become stressed less easily than a pet who wandered the streets, looking for its next meal for the first year of its life.

No matter what your pet's background, there are steps you can take to reduce its stress levels, and maybe lower your own in the process. Here are some suggestions:

Recognize the wild thing in your pet. Many cats and dogs have, to varying degrees, an innate drive to chase, catch, and kill prey. I'm not suggesting that you practice a catch and release program so your cat can stalk her own live mice, but there are acceptable ways to incorporate your pet's prey drive into your household.

One of our cats loves to chase a feather attached to a flexible rod — it's a game that lets him practice stalking, and entertains him and my youngest daughter, at the other end of the rod, for hours. You can buy a similar gizmo or make your own, or simply drag a piece of string across the floor for kitty to chase. (Always use a toy when playing with your cat, however. If you allow him to stalk your hand, he may see it as prey, and inflict painful bites or scratches.)

For dogs, consider activities that let them release energy and use their natural instincts. Hounds may enjoy lure coursing, for example — a sport in which the dog chases a plastic "bunny" over the twists and turns of rugged terrain. Other breeds may benefit from tracking lessons, which teach them to follow a scent trail. Try and find activities that allow your pet to do what it was bred for, or at the very least seems to enjoy, and you'll provide a natural outlet for instincts that might otherwise be used to catch and kill your shoes.

If it's possible, you might want to consider getting another cat or dog as a companion to your pet. My two German Shepherd Dogs stalk and tackle each other while playing, a great release of energy and instinct.

My English Setter, Parker, likes to curl up for a nap behind my desk. It's his spot and off-limits to my children.

Give your pet a room of its own. Not literally, of course, unless you are Bill Gates and have room to spare. But all pets need a place to go when the world is just too much for them. For dogs, it can be a crate, a dog bed, or even a towel. Cats may prefer a raised carpeted box, a cubbyhole, or space under a guest bed.

Whatever you use, make sure that pets and people alike realize the space is just for Fluffy or Fido. That means it's off-limits to children, guests, and, aside from the occasional cleaning, you.

Giving pets their own space has lots of advantages for everyone. Picture this: it's a typical night at your house. The television is blaring, your spouse is rushing to get dinner ready, and the kids are screaming and running around. What's the smart pet to do? Promptly remove paws and whiskers to the safest spot he knows — his crate.

When our children were small, they would follow our German Shepherd Dog Jano from room to room, petting, brushing, and playing with him. He'd put up with their attentions good-naturedly for most of the day, then take a break by retreating to his bed. The girls knew they couldn't disturb him there, and Jano knew he was safe until he was ready to play again.

The other benefit of giving your pet a safe place comes when you are traveling or visiting friends. A crate, box, or even blanket can provide a sense of security and reduce stress in an unfamiliar setting.

Friends of mine have trained their dog Troy to recognize a large towel as his special spot. Because he's well-mannered and friendly, Troy is often a requested guest at parties. Whenever his owners think that he's had too much excitement or cheese dip, they simply spread the towel out and tell him to settle down. Troy is content in this spot for as long as the festivities last.

Train, train, train. Some pet owners think that obedience training is a waste of time for animals that aren't "show pets."

The truth is, training that uses positive techniques can give your pet the tools it needs to fit into your household, and can tremendously enhance your relationship with it.

Pets need to know what their place is, and where they fit into your life. Dogs in particular are pack animals, and training can help establish you as the "head dog." Plus, training gives you an activity that you can do together, and helps your pet to focus more on you.

Finally, training can help your pet have a social life. If your dog is well-behaved and friendly, if your friends know he can be trusted not to steal potato chips off the table or to climb on the sofa, he'll be a welcome guest — not a forlorn face at the window as you drive away, leaving him home once again.

Be consistent. The flip side of training is follow-up, and if you want to have a successful relationship with your pet, it's essential. It's confusing for pets when the rules are always changing. If you shoo your cat off the kitchen counter one day, then let him roam around on it the next, then yell at him the third day, what message does that send? Certainly not the one you want.

Pets get stressed when they don't know what you expect. The only way to make sure they understand the rules is to consistently and fairly enforce them. Doing so makes it clear that you are the boss, that your word is law, and that pets can expect you to behave in a certain way time after time.

As much as our creatures may care about us, they are much like two-year-old human kids — they have their own best interests at heart. If they think, based on past experiences with you, that they can get away with stealing the rump roast off the table, then that's what they are going to do.

One of our clients has a firm rule — no dogs on the furniture. The husband is a stickler about this, and when he feels the first pressure of a paw sneaking up on the bed, he promptly removes it.

The wife, however, is more likely to roll over and ignore it, particularly if the stealth attack is happening late at night. The result? Their dog sleeps on the floor when the husband is home, and hogs the bed the rest of the time.

Don't nag. Remember when you were a kid, and you had to take out the trash? Your mom might have reminded you two, three, or five times to do it. If you were like most kids, eventually you just tuned her out. Your mom might have become frustrated, yelled at you, or decided it was simpler just to do it herself. The end result? Your mom was unhappy, and you were annoyed for getting yelled at.

But what happened if your mom asked you just once to take out the trash, and when you didn't do it right away, she docked your allowance? The next time she asked you to do

Introducing new pets to each other can be stressful. Make sure you do it slowly.

something, you probably hustled to get it done. You knew what she wanted, and you knew there would be consequences if you didn't follow through.

Dogs and cats don't get allowances, but they do get praise, attention, and maybe even treats from you. If your pet doesn't listen when you give it a command the first time, and you know he knows what you want him to do, correct him. By this I don't mean you should whack him over the head with a newspaper — if your dog is attuned to you, saying "bad dog" or simply looking at him sternly should be enough.

The rule should be "one command, one action." Say your pet's name clearly and distinctly, follow it with the command, and expect to see results. Nagging gets you nothing but a pet that doesn't respect or understand you.

A word of warning — pets aren't born knowing how to sit, lay down, or stay off the furniture. As a responsible pet owner, it's your job to make sure they know the rules BEFORE you give the command. Simply putting Fido in the sit position once or twice, or swatting Fluffy off the couch isn't enough. It can take hundreds of repetitions before your pet truly understands what you want when you ask it to do something. Only when you have put that time in, and are sure your pet knows what you want, should you correct it.

People stop me all the time to admire my dog Jano. They always say the same thing: "You're so lucky to have such a well-trained dog. My pet would never behave like that." Luck has nothing to do with it, but hard work and consistency do. If you want a well-behaved pet that you can go places with you, and that you can have a relationship with, you have to work at it.

Turn your pet into a party animal. I'm not suggesting that you strap a birthday hat on your pet, just that you help him become more social. A social pet is one that gets along with both people and other animals, and a pet becomes social by having a wide range of positive experiences.

Take your pet places with you, and introduce him to your friends, to your family, to your car, as early and as often as possible. Keep it simple at first: the world can be overwhelming to a puppy, kitten, or even an older pet that hasn't gotten out much. Walk your dog or cat around the block on a leash, and let it stop to sniff and explore. Later, when he's comfortable with this, try taking him to meet people outside of the mall, grocery store, or local school.

Before your pet gets to meet the cute dog or cat next door, get your vet's okay. Young animals need vaccinations to protect them from potentially fatal diseases, and before they receive them, it's not a good idea to expose them to other animals.

Once your pet is set with his shots, let him meet as many friendly creatures as possible. Keep both animals on a leash at first, and correct any signs of aggressiveness at once in a stern voice. For dogs, watch their body language — if the tail is in the air, the head is low, and the animal looks as if it's bowing, it's indicating that it wants to play. For cats, hissing, agitated tail swishing, or serious stalking may portend a fight in the immediate future — gentle sniffing or tapping at each other with paws are better signs.

Some cities have "dog parks" where your pet can go to meet others and play. If it's handled the right way, this can be a lot of fun for both of you. Before you go, make sure your dog is up-to-date on his shots, and that you've got enough verbal control over him to feel comfortable letting him run. If not, keep him on the leash.

Cars are also a part of the socialization process, and should be introduced gradually. Start by letting your pet hop in and sit in the back while the car is parked. If you'll be using a carrier or restraint system, spend a few minutes letting him get familiar with it on a day when you are not planning on going anywhere. Once he's comfortable, gradually build up the length of your trips.

Make sure that your car trips aren't just to the vet's or groomer's. Go to the park for a run, to the pet shop for a treat, to a friend's to visit. This way, your pet will come to associate travel with fun, happy things, and it will always be an enjoyable experience for him.

By thoughtfully exposing your pet to a wide range of stimuli, you can help him handle new situations with confidence, not stress.

Stuck to you like Elmer's glue is how your pet should be. I'm not talking about a nervous, neurotic animal that hides behind you when the doorbell rings; I'm referring to the confident pet who looks to you for direction, support, and guidance.

When you've developed a bond of trust with your pet, you will automatically be the most important thing in his world. If he's confident in you, he'll be much less stressed in unfamiliar or threatening surroundings.

Jake, an Airedale, is my favorite example of this. When I met him, Jake was a puppy, owned by a young man who was living with his parents. Over the course of the next two years, Jake and his owner moved into an apartment where there were several other animals, to a house by the sea, and finally to a co-op in New York. Those are a lot of changes for anyone, but especially for a pet. Throughout it all, Jake remained calm and confident, whether chasing waves or frolicking in Central Park. His focus was on his owner, and as long as he was there, Jake was happy.

His owner put a lot of time and effort into building this type of relationship between dog and human. He worked on training, so that Jake would be welcome wherever he went. He was consistent, so that Jake knew eating shoes wasn't allowed no matter where they lived. And most importantly, he made Jake a part of his life. He took him on walks, to car rides, even to family gatherings.

This type of friendship with your pet doesn't develop

overnight, but it's worth the investment. It means that both you and your pet can have a fuller, more complete relationship together — and isn't that the whole purpose of having a pet?

Don't worry, be happy! Pets are very sensitive to your mood. If you are tense and unhappy, it's likely that they will be too. Think of pets as little fur-covered mirrors — when you look at them, what do you see? If you want a calm, easygoing pet, you need to be a calm, easy-going owner. If you are always running around, tense and irritable, it's a good bet your pet will be that way too.

Think of staying calm for your pet as returning a favor: studies have shown that owning pets may help lower blood

The very presence of pets can help our health. Having Buddy around always puts me in a good mood.

pressure and cholesterol levels. Pet owners may also visit their doctors less frequently, and be more likely to survive a heart attack.

Recognize your pet's individuality. His breeding, background, and environment have combined to make him a unique animal. He may love to chase a ball, or hate to swim in the water. He may "talk" at all hours, or be the strong, silent type. Whatever his habits, recognize that he's an individual, with his own likes, dislikes, and desires. If you can identify these things and channel them correctly, you can help your pet — and yourself — live a happier life.

A young woman I know named Linda adopted a cute ball of fluff from the local shelter. Christened Moxie because of his spunk, the puppy grew up to be a terror. He was constantly whining, digging holes in the backyard, and chasing whatever moved. He was always in trouble, and always stressed.

Linda did some research on her pet, and learned that he was probably part Border Collie — a breed with a keen intelligence and capacity to work. Just standing around all day watching the grass grow was driving this type A personality dog crazy — he needed a way to focus his energy. Linda enrolled in a class that taught dog owners how to do frisbee routines — dramatic leaps, bounds, and flips set to music.

A few months later, most of Moxie's undesirable habits have stopped. The frisbee classes, combined with the practice sessions, help Moxie burn off energy while engaging his mind. The result is a happier, more relaxed dog. Because her dog is better-behaved, Linda is happier too. A little bit of research and thought paid off big for both pet and owner.

Feed your pet well. If you've ever tried to lose weight quickly, you've probably experienced the dieter's blues — you become irritable, tired, maybe even light-headed. This reaction is your body's way of telling you that you aren't getting enough calories and nutrients.

Unlike us, our pets can't walk into the kitchen and whip up a well-balanced meal. They depend on us for that. And if we aren't feeding them correctly, they suffer.

In the wild, animals often eat all or most of their kill. Fur, feathers, bones, and intestines provide valuable nutrients, help keep their coats glossy, and give them the energy they need to survive another day.

The best way to ensure a well-balanced diet for your pet is to educate yourself. Read books, talk with your veterinarian, and ask other pet owners with healthy, glowing animals what they feed. I refuse to feed my pets — or any animals — food that I wouldn't eat myself.

Mrs. Allen's SHED -STOP was originally consumed by people, not pets. It's derived from an old family formula that was used by my grandfather, a farmer who lived in a small village near Transylvania. My grandfather had a long, full head of hair — and the sheepdogs he owned had thick, luxurious fur. They were so healthy, and shed so rarely, that they were allowed to live in the house — an unheard of privilege for animals in those days.

The animals looked so good because they were eating the same secret formula that my grandfather was. It was a mix of herbs, oils, and vitamins, and it's the same formula that we use to make Mrs. Allen's SHED-STOP today. It provides the vital ingredients necessary for your pet's overall health and well-being.

Feeding it won't cause stress at dinnertime, either. It's highly palatable, and easy to use by simply mixing into your pet's food. It's also recommended by veterinarians.

While not a cure-all, SHED-STOP can help improve your pet's nutrition, making him a healthier — and happier — animal. It can also help reduce shedding and skin problems, which can make your life as a pet owner easier — reducing stress for both of you.

Equipment for de-stressing your pet:

- crate or carrier

- patience

- consistency

Questions to ask:

Does my pet fully understand the rules I expect him to live by? If not, why not? In most cases, the problem isn't with the pet — it's with the owner. What do you need to do to make sure your pet knows what you want from him? Understanding what's expected can do a lot to reduce stress.

Are the rules that pertain to my pet consistently enforced? By "consistent" I mean "every time." If you don't want the cat on the counters, you have to remove her from them — every time she's on them, no matter how far away the counters are from you, or how tired you may be.

What is my pet's energy level like? Is he full of energy, constantly in motion? Or is he a couch potato? Burning off excess energy can help to relax your pet. Consider taking him for regularly scheduled walks, runs, or hikes. You may also want to investigate other activities, such as frisbee, or agility. Even regularly scheduled "play dates," with other pets can help him release energy and reduce stress.

What types of triggers stress my pet? Other animals, thunderstorms, loud noises, strangers, are all common triggers. Some are easy to identify and fix. Others may require more work.

Can I expose my pet to these triggers in a safe environment, in gradual degrees, to reduce his anxiety over them? For example, if your cat gets stressed when riding in the car, try placing her, in a carrier, in the motionless car for a few moments each day. Gradually increase her exposure, and associate it with positive things — feeding, grooming, spending time with you. After enough time has passed that she no longer cries when the car is motionless, leave the car running for a short period of time. Progress to short trips, such as around the block, before attempting longer ones. The key to success is patience — although it's tempting, don't jump ahead at the first sign she has relaxed.

If the problem is too big for me to fix, and involves behavior that is a threat to me, my pet, or other people or animals, who can help? Your veterinarian or trainer may be able to assist you, or may be able to suggest someone who can.

Top 10 Tips

1. **Recognize the wild thing in your pet.** Pets aren't people in furry little suits. They are animals, with animal needs. Forcing your pet to suppress those needs can cause stress.

2. **Give your pet a positive way to release energy.** Exercise is a great way to reduce nervous energy. Encourage your pet to chase a ball, bat a toy mouse around, or participate in organized events such as agility.

3. **Give your pet a room of its own.** A crate can be a big comfort to a stressed-out animal. It's a quiet place he can retreat to whenever the world is overwhelming.

4. **Take training seriously.** Training spells out the rules for pets, and pets are happiest when they know exactly what's expected of them.

5. **Be consistent.** Don't change the rules from day-to-day.

6. **Don't nag.** The rule should be "one command, one action."

7. **Turn your pet into a party animal.** Expose him to different situations, and make each one a positive experience.

8. **Don't worry, be happy!** Pets pick up on our moods very easily. If you are upset and tense, your pet may be too.

9. **Recognize your pet's individuality.** His breeding, background, and environment have combined to make him a unique animal. Identifying and channeling his likes and dislikes can help your pet live a happier life.

10. **Feed your pet well.** Good nutrition can help him to be a happier and healthier animal.

9

Travel Time

Pets can be the perfect traveling companions. They don't demand to stop at factory shopping outlets. They pass by fast-food joints without whining. You'll never hear a dog criticize your driving skills, and even the most finicky cat isn't likely to debate your choice of routes. And whether you prefer Mozart or major league baseball games, the radio is guaranteed to stay on the station you select.

But traveling with pets isn't all life in the fast lane — a successful journey requires some advance planning. What happens when the hotel you've chosen refuses to let Fluffy in the door? Will well-behaved Fido revolt after six straight hours of sitting still in the car? What if you can't find your pet's brand of food on the road, and he won't eat anything else?

Whether you are planning on taking a plane, train, or automobile, here are some suggestions that can make the trip safer and more enjoyable for both you and your four-legged companion:

Show some restraint. Restraint systems, such as a carrier or crate, provide your pet with an additional measure of safety when traveling in the car. If there's an accident, your pet won't go tumbling about. If someone opens the car door unexpectedly, he won't be running wild across the highway. And if your pet gets sick, the mess is contained and can be easily cleaned. Best of all, you won't find 100 pounds of friendly fur in your lap while trying to change lanes, or napping under your brake pedal when you need to stop.

Crates and carriers are required for most pets who are traveling on an airplane, so it makes sense to acclimate them in advance. If you are positive that your pet will never, ever fly the friendly skies, and you don't want to use a crate in your car, consider a harness system for dogs. It works on the same principle as a seat belt, and can be purchased at many pet stores.

If neither the crate nor the harness will work in your situation, at least train your pet not to enter or exit an automobile until you give it the command. Not only can this save your pet's life, it can also prevent damage to any important documents or dry-cleaned clothes that might be stretched across the seat of your car.

This type of training is still not a substitute for the safety of a crate or carrier. One well-behaved Rottweiler of my acquaintance took a dislike to something he saw out the window of the car one day. Without so much as a bark, he launched himself out of the window and onto the road — damaging both hips in the process. His recovery period was long, but fortunately, not as long as it would have been if the person driving behind him hadn't swerved in time.

Start slowly. If you are planning to drive cross country, don't simply load Fido into the car and start your engine. Spend a little time getting your pet used to the car in advance — when it's not moving. You may want to feed him his dinner in the crate in a motionless car, for example. Once he's comfortable, drive around the block a few times.

Find a fun destination — a friend's house, a local park, a store that allows pets to visit — and go there a few times. If your pet only associates the car with trips to the vet or the groomer, he may resist any attempts to travel. When he's mastered short trips and seems comfortable, build up the length of driving time.

If your pet experiences motion sickness, talk with your vet. He or she may recommend medication that can help. There are also a host of home remedies, ranging from feeding minute amounts of ginger prior to the trip to covering the bottom of the crate with brown paper bags to ensuring your pet has a window view. If you hear of one that's safe and sounds reason able, give it a try.

Watch the weather. Never, under any circumstances, leave an unattended animal in the car in warm weather. Even the balmiest spring days can be uncomfortable for pets trapped in a vehicle. If you have any doubt about the temperature, leave your pet in the house, park the car in full sun, roll up the windows, and sit there for a few minutes. If it's even remotely uncomfortable for you, it's too hot for your pet. If the weather is cool enough to leave your pet in the car, always leave the windows cracked open to allow adequate ventilation.

When driving, watch your pet closely. If he seems to be panting or is restless, turn up the air conditioning. If he's sitting in the back away from the car's vents, he may not be getting a sufficient flow of cool air.

A crate can provide a safe, quiet place to rest when traveling.

Keep in mind, too, that many airlines have temperature restrictions for flying pets. If the weather is too hot or too cold, your pet may be grounded. Call in advance to discuss the airline's rules, and be prepared to take alternative steps, such as boarding your pet, should the weather not cooperate on the day of your flight.

I.D., please. If you are traveling with your pet, make sure he's easily identifiable if you are separated. Identification tags should contain your name and phone number. You might also want to have the phone number of a friend or family member on the tag as well, in case you aren't able to check your answering machine messages from a remote site. The tag should be affixed to a collar that's snug but not too tight. Or better yet, get a nylon or leather collar with your pet's name and your phone number sewn on, since tags can and often do come off. Avoid leaving training or "choke" collars on your pet for any length of time — they can strangle him if they get caught on a branch, piece of furniture, or another animal.

Tattoos or microchips are other I.D. options. If you choose to tattoo your pet, make the number and name something that's easily identifiable, such as your phone number. If your microchip company will allow it, provide more than one phone number. If you are traveling and your pet is lost, you won't necessarily be able to return home to answer calls.

Check in for a checkup. Keep in mind that airlines require pets to have a certificate of health from a veterinarian before flying. The certificate, which states that the pet is in good health and up-to-date on all his shots, must have been issued within a 10-day period of the flight.

If you are driving, you don't need the certificate, but you might want to have it anyway. In a pinch, it can serve as a proof of ownership. In addition, it lists all the animal's vaccination information in one spot. If you choose not to have the exam done, be sure to carry vaccination information with you, particularly that for rabies and distemper.

Research the region. If you'll be traveling out of your immediate area, check with your veterinarian to see what precautions, if any, you may need to take. Diseases and illnesses can vary geographically. If you are traveling to an area where Lyme Disease is prevalent, for example, he may recommend a Lyme vaccination for your pet.

If the weather is much different at your destination, consider bringing appropriate gear for your pet. If you'll be hiking in snowy weather, or along roads where there may be rock salt, a sweater and boots for your dog may be a good idea. It may not be the most dignified solution, but if it keeps your pet warm, and protects his feet, who cares?

Be prepared. Accidents and injuries don't just happen at home — they can take the fun out of your journey if you're not careful. To protect your pet, keep the phone number of your veterinarian close at hand. If there's an emergency, you can call for advice or assistance.

A sturdy collar and lead can help keep your pet safe when traveling.

A first-aid kit for your pet can also be beneficial. At the minimum, it should contain
- a soft muzzle (pets that are injured and panicked may bite)
- an antibacterial ointment or spray
- clean towels
- styptic powder to control bleeding from minor cuts
- bandages
- a splint
- cotton balls
- alcohol
- scissors
- gauze
- flea and tick protection
- medication for motion sickness (discuss what to use with your vet).

Hotel, motel, or campground? No matter what type of sleeping accommodations you plan to use during your trip, it's a good idea to phone ahead to make sure they accept pets. Some places refuse to allow pets; others require an additional deposit; still others have no problems with well-behaved animals.

If your pet is crate or carrier trained, let the hotel or motel know that you will confine your pet when you are not in the room. And no matter where you stay, be sure to clean up after your pet, both outside on walks or inside the room. Anything else is irresponsible pet ownership.

Hide and seek, anyone? Like small children, pets get bored if the focus of the trip is oriented solely toward human adults. To break the monotony for them, plan a few pet-oriented activities. Hiking, walking on the beach, or socializing with other animals can all be fun for both pets and their owners. In addition, these activities can help your pet burn off excess energy, which can result in a quiet, stress-free trip for you.

If stopping for these types of activities is out of the question, at least pack a few new toys to eliminate boredom. A new chew bone, a wind-up toy, or a squeaky mouse can keep your pet occupied and out of your hair.

Back to school. A refresher training course may be in order before you leave on your trip. Even the most well-behaved pet can forget his manners in new surroundings. Spend some time practicing common commands with your pet before you leave, but don't just school in your house or backyard. Take your pet to the types of situations he's likely to encounter on your trip. A crowded sidewalk, a supermarket parking lot, or even an unfamiliar park can present plenty of temptations for your pet — a perfect situation for training.

If you are staying with friends or relatives on your trip, make sure that rules are consistently enforced. If your pet isn't allowed to sleep on the furniture at home, don't give him any ideas by letting him nap on your host's bed.

Hold the pickles. One of the pleasures of traveling is exploring new foods. Unfortunately, it's one joy your pet shouldn't share. Experimenting with new foods while traveling can give your pet diarrhea, constipation, an upset stomach, or lead to finicky eating.

On trips that will only last a few days, play it safe by packing a supply of your pet's favorite foods, as well as several jugs of his drinking water. If you will be traveling for an extended period of time, it may be more practical to purchase new food, gradually switching your pet over to it.

Well-meaning friends and relatives can also sabotage your pet's diet. One Sheltie I knew was overjoyed whenever the family traveled to Grandma's house, because Grandma insisted on cooking him his own omelette every morning. Likewise, a Rhodesian Ridgeback was always happy to make the two-hour trip to visit his owner's grandmother, who was a little forgetful. Once there, he would park himself in front of the cookie drawer. Every time Grandma passed, she'd feel sorry for the "poor starving dog," and slip him a Fig Newton, unaware that she had just done the same thing a short while before.

Politely remind your hosts of your pet's dietary restrictions. If that doesn't work, you may have to look the other way for a few days, and put your pet on a diet when you return home.

At least you can be sure your pet is receiving the necessary vitamins and nutrients if you carry a supply of Mrs. Allen's SHED-STOP on your trip. In addition, the great taste of this all-natural supplement can help make unfamiliar food more palatable to your pet. And by eliminating "nuisance" shedding, Mrs. Allen's SHED-STOP will help make your pet welcome anywhere!

Equipment for traveling:

- Collar with I.D. tags

- leash or harness

- crate

- water

- food

- treats

- first-aid kit

- your vet's phone number

- record of shots

- any medication your pet takes

- a blanket or bed

- plastic bags for cleanup duty

Steps to take before your trip:

1. **Check with your vet to make sure your pet has the neces-sary vaccinations for the area in which you will be traveling.** Record information here.

2. **Locate pet-friendly establishments in which to stay on your journey.** There are several books on the market that deal specifically with this topic. The internet is also a great resource.

3. **Research pet parks, shows, or other activities the two of you can enjoy.**

Top 10 Tips

1. **Show some restraint.** If you are traveling, make sure your pet has a secure seat. That means using a crate, carrier, or harness.

2. **Start slowly.** Acclimate your pet to the car gradually. Get him used to sitting in it without the engine running. Build up to short trips, then gradually increase the distance.

3. **Watch the weather.** Never leave your pet unattended in the car when the weather's warm.

4. **I.D., please.** Make sure your pet can be identified in case you are separated from him during your trip. A sturdy collar with tags is essential; tattoos or microchips can also help.

5. **Check in for a check-up.** If you'll be flying, the airlines require a certificate of health from your veterinarian. The certificate can also be useful if you are traveling by car as well.

6. **Research the region.** New areas to explore can mean new hazards for your pet, such as Lyme Disease. Know what the potential problems are before you go.

7. **Be prepared.** A first-aid kit for your pet is essential.

8. **Hotel, motel, or campground?** No matter where you are planning to stay, call ahead to ensure they accept pets.

9. **Hide and seek, anyone?** Just like little kids, pets can get bored and rambunctious on long trips. Plan some pet-centered activities, such as hiking, to let them blow off steam.

10. **Hold the pickles.** Miles from home isn't the time for your pet to try out new treats. Stick with familiar food to avoid stomach upset, loose stools, gas, and other unpleasant problems.

10

Holiday Hangovers

Poisonous plants, treacherous trees, hazardous travel — it may sound like an action adventure film, but it's actually a description of the holidays from your pet's point of view. For humans, the food, decorations, and excitement surrounding the holidays add to the festive feel. Unfortunately, for our pets it's a different story.

Too many table scraps can spell indigestion. Tinsel and other ornaments, which often dangle at a pet-tempting level, can be hazards, as can certain plants associated with the holidays. And the departures from routine, the new faces, the later hours that we associate with fun times at the holidays can create stress in your pet.

With two small children, the holidays at our house are a big deal. We trim the tree, bake cookies, attend parties, and host events for family and friends. But I'm careful to include our pets in the celebration too — not just by buying new chew toys and catnip, but by making sure they get the attention and care that they need. The following are steps I've used to make the holidays safer and more enjoyable for my four-legged friends. I hope you find them helpful, too:

No puppies for presents. And no kittens either. It's every child's fantasy to get a warm, wriggling puppy or kitten as a gift. Unfortunately, the holidays are probably the worst time to bring home a pet. Many reputable breeders refuse to sell animals over the holidays for this reason.

New pets need some quiet time, as well as a regular routine, to help them get accustomed to their new home. Quiet time and Christmas, or other holidays, is an oxymoron in most houses. Bright lights, many faces, screaming, shouting, late nights, trips to Grandma's house, no time for walks, no time to change the litter box ... this is not the environment in which to introduce a new pet.

If you've got your heart set on giving a pet for the holidays, make it a stuffed one instead — perhaps one in a potential pet's image, with a date for the real one to arrive attached. It's also a good idea to give books on pet care to the child as well. That way, he or she can spend the days before the new animal arrives learning how to care for it. Pick a date with your breeder in advance, preferably one several days after the holidays, and let the child go with you to bring the pet home.

Pets aren't a no-no as presents for just children. Even

Our holiday photo wouldn't be complete without a very important member of our family — Jano.

adults shouldn't receive pets as presents — if you think Aunt Ethel is lonely and would like the company of a kitten, it's better to ask in advance than surprise her with one. Although dogs and cats can be wonderful companions, there's a certain degree of care and commitment that's required. Not everyone is willing or able to provide these things, particularly around the holidays.

Be good, for goodness sake. Like little kids, pets seem to be particularly rambunctious during the holidays. There are just so many opportunities to misbehave: appetizers to swipe off the coffee table, Christmas trees to climb, guests to greet with a cold snout or muddy paws .... All these distractions make a perfect opportunity for refresher training.

Try to schedule a training session for a few minutes every morning. Obedience training at this point will do two things: give your pet some much-needed attention during all of the holiday hullabaloo, and provide some reinforcement on what type of behavior is acceptable.

If you are tempted to bend the rules around the holidays, think twice: once you've given the okay, your pet will expect that waiver to continue. If the rule is no dogs on the furniture, for example, but on Christmas Eve you decide to let Fido on the sofa as a special treat, he'll want to be up there next week as well.

One of our biggest rules is that no dogs are allowed in the dining room while we eat. All of our animals know this and are comfortable waiting in the living room for us to finish our meal. One Christmas dinner, however, my mother invited them into the room, and surreptitiously fed them table scraps. Our German Shepherd's head is at table level, and every now and then someone's dinner roll disappeared.

It took me a week to get them to obey the original rule: once they'd figured out what they were missing, the dogs no longer wanted to wait patiently outside when they could be eating with us.

Pet-proof the house. There are a host of hazards around the holidays. They include:

Electrical cords. Playful kittens and cats can't resist an extension cord snaking through the room, but clawing or biting it could result in electrocution. Make sure cords are secured and out of reach.

Trees and trimmings. Christmas trees are too tempting for even the best-behaved pet to ignore. For kittens and cats, they are a perfect size to climb or claw. And all pets are fascinated by the tinsel and ornaments, any one of which could cause major internal injury if swallowed. For safety's sake, secure your tree behind closed doors, particularly if you have cats. (A baby gate will serve to keep most dogs out.) If that's impossible, provide strict supervision for pets around the tree, and make sure it is securely held in its stand. If you must go out and leave the tree accessible to pets, unplug any lights, remove low-hanging ornaments, and avoid decorating with tinsel or angel hair, which could cause intestinal problems if swallowed.

Impractical presents. Ribbon, yarn, string, and other decorative touches on gifts may look attractive, but can cause problems if they are ingested. Keep pets away from gifts unless they are supervised.

Poisonous plants. Poinsettias, mistletoe, and other holiday plants, such as bulb arrangements, could be toxic if swallowed by pets. Keep them out of your pet's way, and secure them behind closed doors if you must go out.

Diet dilemma. It's tempting to give Fido or Fluffy special treats around the holidays, such as poultry fat, rich gravy, or chicken bones. But any of these foods can trigger intestinal problems, ranging from inflammation of the pancreas and intestine to internal puncture wounds.

That's not to say you can't give your pet special goodies, but be careful. A few scraps of meat or chicken won't hurt, but

Our treats make a special holiday gift for pets and owners alike!

skin, fat, and bone can do serious damage. One good rule is to only feed your pet food you would eat yourself. A little meat juice or chicken broth over kibble is a wonderful treat, for example, but avoid large pieces of gristle.

For dogs, knuckle bones can provide hours of chewing fun. These bones can be purchased at your meat counter. Never give poultry bones, which can splinter in the animal's stomach. And for other treat ideas for both dogs and cats, check out some of the new recipe books written solely for four-legged gourmands. (Every year I make a big batch of Pets n' People Snacks that everyone can share, and give them as stocking stuffers to my friends' pets. They're easy to make and a big hit.)

Practical presents. Pets don't want designer doggie outfits or deluxe litter boxes for the holidays — the gift they appreciate most is extra time with you. A long walk, a belly-rubbing session, a few extra scratches behind the ear are what the holidays are all about to them.

Still, it's tempting to make sure there's a gift with your pet's name on it under the tree. At our house, all of our animals have their own packages to open, under supervision. If you are planning on a gift for your pet, toys that will keep him busy during the holidays are a good bet. For dogs, veterinarian-approved chew toys are a great idea. (Other types of toys can splinter with rough usage, causing internal problems.)

Avoid tennis balls for big dogs, who can take them apart, swallow them, or have them become wedged in their throats, cutting off air supply. Oversized solid rubber balls may be a better choice.

For cats, a new scratching post makes a stress-free present. Another idea is an edible garden — grass grown just for your pet. Cats love to nibble on green things, and giving them their own garden can help reduce wear and tear on your house plants while keeping cats safe. Check with your local pet shop or garden supply center, both of which may grow special cat grass blends. Otherwise, rye grass seed is acceptable.

Traveling tips. If you'll be traveling with your pet this holiday, a few simple precautions can make the trip safer and more enjoyable for both of you. First, make sure your pet wears a collar with an I.D. tag. The tag should have your address, your phone number, and if possible the number of a friend, family member, breeder, kennel, or vet. If you become separated and someone finds your pet, the second number increases the chances that someone who is home will be contacted.

Next, bring a supply of food and water. Many pets may refuse to drink from an unfamiliar water supply, or may develop an upset stomach. And don't forget Mrs. Allen's SHED-STOP! Holidays are a stressful time for pets, and keeping them on my supplement can help reduce shedding caused by stress. In addition, if you are traveling and run out of food, SHED-STOP helps disguise the unfamiliar taste of a new brand.

If you will be traveling by car, take a few precautions in advance. Cats should travel secured in a box or carrier. Dogs should be strapped into a safety harness or secured in a crate.

Never let your dog travel untethered in the back of a pickup — a sudden stop or swerve could send him flying. Even tethered dogs have minimum protection in the case of an accident. If your pet can't travel with you in the cab, consider leaving him home.

If you will be flying, check with the airline about travel restrictions. Some airlines refuse to fly animals in extremely hot or cold weather. Although this can protect your pet from overheating or freezing, it can play havoc with your travel schedule if you arrive at the airport and are told Fido won't be flying today. Have a backup plan: a friend who can retrieve your animal from the airport and keep him over the holidays.

Also talk with your vet about the best way to handle the stress of flying. Some vets will prescribe a tranquilizer, while others feel that the drug can be more traumatic to the animal than the flight itself. And don't forget to get a certificate of health from your vet before flying — the airlines won't let your pet on without it.

Plan in advance. If you need to board your pet over the holidays, keep in mind that it's a busy time for kennels. Make reservations well in advance. Find out what immunizations the kennel requires, and if the place is unfamiliar to your pet, consider bringing him by in advance to get acquainted.

A pet sitter is another option if you'll be leaving your animals behind during the holidays. Make sure you introduce the person and your pet well in advance of your departure. One acquaintance of mine left on a trip, only to receive a frantic call: her dog refused to let the sitter into the house! Luckily, the owner's mother lived nearby and was able to save the day, but it could have been a disaster. A little foresight and time can reduce the chance that this will happen to you.

No room at the inn. Around the holidays, it seems that our animals are always underfoot. One solution is to provide them with a safe space of their own. A crate can be a big help when animals are overtired or just in the way. Toss a few treats inside and let them get away from the noise and excitement. Crates and carriers can be a boon when traveling, too — they provide a safe, familiar place in strange surroundings.

Stay calm. One of my favorite holiday stories revolves around Thanksgiving. A woman who owned several dogs was preparing a holiday feast, complete with an oversized turkey. Just as she announced that dinner was ready, a loud crash was heard. Through the doors, the expectant guests caught a glimpse of the regal bird sitting on the kitchen floor— with several dogs surrounding it.

There was a pause.

"Harold," the woman called to her husband. "Bring out the other turkey." She then turned to her guests, excused herself, and entered the kitchen. Fifteen minutes later, a bird reappeared on the platter. Only the closest of inspections revealed that it was missing a few parts.

Not every holiday disaster is as big as this one, but having a sense of humor and being flexible can go a long way toward saving the day, with or without the help of our four-legged friends!

Try It Yourself

Equipment that can be especially useful around the holidays:

- a crate or carrier

- several new pet toys

- a first aid-kit

- a baby gate

- plain white rice for pets who overindulge

Questions to ask:

What holiday hazards exist in my home? Sit on the floor at your pet's height. What looks especially tempting — the cookies at muzzle level, the glass ornaments, the lights dangling from the tree? Record hazards here.

How can I prevent my pet from getting hurt? Some solutions are obvious — cookies can be covered or moved to a higher spot. Others may take more thought. Can you put the Christmas tree in a room with a door that can be shut? Would a baby gate keep pets out? Can lights be unplugged when not in use?

How can I include my pets in the holidays? Pets don't need gifts to feel good — an early-morning walk, a late night snuggle, some quality time with you are all that's required. Too often, pets get shunted to the side during busy times, and regular routines, such as obedience sessions, get dropped. But it's during these high-stress times that attention is especially necessary.

What are some safe, edible treats my pet can enjoy? Be creative — what about ice cubes made from frozen chicken or beef broth? A small amount of peanut butter in a beef marrow bone? A pot of rye grass? Although people food in small doses won't hurt your pet, too much can make him sick. But everyone wants to indulge their animals during the holidays. Now is the time to come up with some safe, healthy alternatives.

Top 10 Tips

1. **No pets for presents.** The holiday season, with all its hustle and bustle, isn't the time to bring a new animal into your house. Hold off until you can give that puppy or kitten the attention he needs.

2. **Be good, for goodness sake.** Low-hanging decorations, rich hors d'oeuvres at nose level, oddly shaped packages to pounce on — the temptations for pets during the holidays are endless. Schedule some extra training time to remind them of the rules.

3. **Be consistent.** If you don't want your 150-pound "lap dog" getting comfortable on the sofa, don't bend the rules around the holidays. Pets don't understand the word "exception."

4. **Pet-proof the house.** Poisonous plants, plugged-in lights, and chocolate bonbons can all prove hazardous to your pet's health. Take a few minutes to identify and eliminate potential holiday dangers.

5. **Diet dilemma.** Rich holiday fare can throw your pet's system out of whack. Stick to his usual food and allow him only healthful treats.

6. **Practical presents.** Pets don't care about how many toys they get. The best gift you can give them is more fun time with you.

7. **Travel time.** If you'll be traveling during the holidays with your pet, make sure he has a sturdy collar with identification tags, and bring food, water, and a first-aid kit.

8. **Plan in advance.** The night before you go out of town isn't the time to be looking for a kennel with a vacancy. Start your search well before the beginning of the holiday season.

9. **No room at the inn.** When your house is overflowing with relatives and friends, your pet can find peace in his own room — his crate.

10. **Stay calm.** Holidays with or without pets can be stressful. Having a sense of humor and being relaxed can go a long way toward saving the day.

Notes

Complete the Perfect Relationship

Developing the perfect relationship with your pet will bring you and your pet much happiness. Selecting the perfect pet care products from the *Mrs. Allen's* SIGNATURE® Collection, will keep your pet looking and feeling its best.

Mrs. Allen's
SIGNATURE®
Collection

I have designed this innovative and practical collection to enhance your experience as a pet owner. From dietary supplements to shampoo, I am sure you'll love them, and as always, they are 100% satisfaction guaranteed. **Contact us today for our free catalog!**

Stabar Enterprises, Inc.

www.mrsallens.com -or-
www.shed-stop.com

P.O. Box 794
Farmington, CT 06032
860-677-1077 • Fax 860-409-7842
Toll Free: 1-800-327-0098
Email: stabar@stabar.com

.